THE SOUL
OF ATLAS

THE SOUL
OF ATLAS

Ayn Rand, Christianity, a Quest
for Common Ground

MARK DAVID HENDERSON

Scripture taken from the HOLY BIBLE, NEW INTERNATIONAL
VERSION®.Copyright © 1973, 1978, 1984 Biblica. Used by
permission of Zondervan. All rights reserved.

Scripture taken from The Message.Copyright © 1993, 1994,
1995, 1996, 2000, 2001, 2002. Used by permission of NavPress
Publishing Group.

Copyright © 2013 by Mark David Henderson
All rights reserved.

ISBN: 1481292048
ISBN-13: 978-1481292047

Without limiting the rights under copyright reserved above,
no part of this publication may be reproduced, stored in or
introduced into a retrieval system, or transmitted, in any form, or
by any means (electronic, mechanical, photocopying, recording, or
otherwise), without the prior written permission of the copyright
owner.

The scanning, uploading, and distribution of this book via
the Internet or via any other means without the permission of
the publisher is illegal and punishable by law. Please purchase
only authorized electronic editions, and do not participate in
or encourage electronic piracy of copyrighted materials. Your
support of the author's rights is appreciated.

While the author has made every effort to provide accurate
telephone numbers and Internet addresses at the time of
publication, neither the publisher nor the author assumes
any responsibility for errors, or for changes that occur after the
publication. Further, the publisher does not have any control over
and does not assume any responsibility for third-party web sites
or their content.

To
Dad and John

CONTENTS

Introduction ix

PART I

INITIATING CONVERSATION:

THE BEGINNING OF A JOURNEY

I   BACK-STORY 3
2   TWO VOICES 17

PART II

TOPICS OF CONVERSATION:

THE LONG ROAD

3   SEX 47
4   MONEY 63
5   CAPITALISM 81
6   REASON 99
7   MEANING 113
8   SELFISHNESS 129
9   JOY 155
10   POWER 171

PART III

FRUITS OF CONVERSATION:

THE DESTINATION

11   WHO IS JOHN GALT? REALLY 193
12   RECONCILIATION 207

Afterward 219
Acknowledgements 223
Notes 225
Bibliography 231
Index 235

INTRODUCTION

People familiar with Ayn Rand do not need a survey to confirm the influence of her writing. Most Christians don't need independent research to illustrate that the Bible has changed the way they live their lives. But without a recent Library of Congress survey, each group may not know just how influential the other may be. In the survey, American readers ranked Ayn Rand's *Atlas Shrugged* the second most influential book in their lives. The Bible is #1.

Both world views exert profound influence on Western culture, politics, economics, social structure, and individual relationships. Yet their influence is seldom recognized and appreciated by the same audience at the same time. It's unlikely that both *Atlas Shrugged* and the Bible were found on any one individual's list. The clash between Ayn Rand's philosophy of Objectivism and Christianity mirrors the war between the religious and secular in Western culture at large. These world views are characterized as foundationally opposed. We don't see many pacifist NRA members or socialist businessmen. Likewise, Christians and Objectivists simply do not run in the same circles. Something about these two domains of thought and praxis, however, is deeply compelling to many Americans. Given that fact, one would imagine there are shelves of books comparing and contrasting these ideologies. In fact, there are not. To date, the Conversation between Objectivism and Christianity has not played out.

As creatures, we are quite attached to the idea that life presents itself in neat, clearly delineated packages: black/white, good/bad, failure/success. But real life rarely affords us that luxury; or perhaps it rarely bores us with such simplicity. This—if I may say so without irony—is a good thing. Sometimes the profound beauty and adventure in life is offered up precisely in shades of gray, or in woven ideas that depict the overlay of multiple, equally complex concepts in a stunning tapestry.

Interception, overlap, simultaneity: these need not demonstrate chaos or compromise; instead, what they often display is richness and, hopefully, depth.

In the past few generations of American society, these two, very distinctive world views have stood as paragons for Faith and Reason themselves. Faith and Reason repeatedly fall prey to our inclination to avert complexity. They can be cartoonishly foisted against one another in simplistic bifurcation. In the twenty-first century, the term "New Atheists" has been coined by journalists to describe some hot, best-selling books—popular authors like Richard Dawkins, Christopher Hitchens, Sam Harris, and Daniel Dennett—that carry the theme "Religion makes no sense." Of course, atheism is not a new idea. For centuries, there have been atheists saying that religion is bad. What's new is the message that respect for religion is bad: that to even be congenial and respectful toward believers is bad; that religion is the worst thing that has ever happened to humankind and it needs to be wiped out. In trying to counter the message of the New Atheism, there are plenty of Christians who simply raise their voices. They do not sympathetically put themselves in the shoes of the doubters. They don't know how to engage in a Conversation. Instead, they heap scorn on the other side. The New Atheists do that too. This Nietzschean power struggle has resulted in alienation and a stalemate.

As with the theist/atheist debate, there seems to be the relentless insistence that Faith and Reason are *merely* opposed to one another, despite history's display of their interplay in symphony. While some people recognize a seamless melding of Faith and Reason, others deny the very prospect. They claim utter sovereignty of one over the other, citing the instances of religion and science or metaphysics and pragmatism clashing. Regardless of these opinions, however, it should be safe to say that Reason and Faith are fundamental drivers of culture and society. Whether one understands Faith as religion or as a mystical hope in Beauty or Love, whether Reason means the empiricism of scientific investigation or the rigor of logic in intelligent rhetoric, we see their interplay in education, politics, entertainment, medicine, and most other realms of life.

Insomuch as Gospel Christianity and Ayn Rand's political philosophy represent seminal forms of Faith and Reason in our culture, why is there such limited analysis in either academic or popular writing of how these world views are similar and how they differ? How is it that a conservative politician could be publically skewered in the media for holding to Randian theories on economics while practicing Catholicism? Moreover, what of his own ambivalence in acknowledging Rand's influence on his thinking? The impulse to apply simplistic characterizations does not allow for a Christian to adhere to Rand's ideas and seems to make the Christian uncomfortable with it as well. Is that a necessary distinction? Furthermore, how would we evaluate whether such a politician is a hypocritical Randian or disingenuous in his Christian beliefs? And why might it even matter? This is a particular example of the kinds of questions this book addresses.

To recognize and comprehend what influences us and others is to function with purpose.

We need to know and it does matter.

It matters how the story of an executed carpenter from first-century Palestine and the story of a political refugee from post-World War I Russia have managed to weave their way into *our* story. It matters because the influences and consequences of these ideas are pervasive in our society in ways overt and subtle; and we need to know what influences us. To recognize and comprehend what influences us and others is to function with purpose. The more purposeful we are in our lives, the more likely we are to achieve what we pursue. And this is not mere utilitarian jargon. "Achievement" can be as varied as developing a kind and loving demeanor, finishing a marathon, or bequeathing a fortune to medical research.

When we know what persuades us, what controls us, and what inspires us, we are able to navigate our lives with intention. Our perspectives develop in concert with *some* principles and in contest against others. This book concerns two of the most profound influencesfor good or for ill—of American ideology in the twentieth century in particular, and investigating those influences is a worthwhile endeavor for anyone interested in how Americans think. Moreover, it is a necessary endeavor in recognizing how these influences affect you, personally.

And so I write a very personal story. The context of my own life makes the conflict and the convergence of Ayn Rand's philosophy and Gospel Christianity unavoidable, as these two world views came to me through the lives of my two fathers. My experiences with these two men illustrate the essence of each world view, the fundamental exclusivity between them, and the ethical conclusions that unite the two men and their beliefs.

Since my parents' divorce and my mother's remarriage when I was eleven years old, my life has been characterized by absorbing, balancing, and reconciling the devout Objectivism of my stepfather, John, and the passionate Christianity of my Dad. One is a champion of rational self-interest, the other a thoughtful man of faith. My intellectual, emotional, and spiritual development played out in the process of *conversations* with these two, brilliant men. Through this book, I invite you to enter into that Conversation so you might consider where these world views vary or unite with your own.

Today, people claim and disclaim both world views with very little comprehension. Arguably, people do this with all kinds of thinking. Unaware, they embrace parts of varying philosophies without regard for consistency. Or, perhaps worse, they dismiss the "other" as misguided and villainous. The merits and influence of these world views mandate more thoughtful consideration. Understanding is a precursor for a meaningful exchange

INTRODUCTION

between these two, influential vantage points, if not from other vantage points, as well. These pages lay the groundwork of understanding as a foundation for a productive dialogue.

Let me say that the Conversation is not only for those, like me, familiar with both world views. Perhaps you have come from the perspective of Dad, as a Christian or even another faith tradition. Perhaps your intellectual background is more sympathetic to John's Objectivism. No matter; keep an open mind. In fact, I would argue that productive interchange requires it. If you come to the Conversation as an atheist or strict rationalist, Dad's well-reasoned Gospel perspective will challenge you. If you approach as a Christian, John's passion and ways of thinking will inspire you to deeper understanding and cause you to question. Finally, if the world view that you articulate differs from both of these men, I envy the adventure that awaits you.

On the way to a comprehensive world view that reconciles what my fathers taught me, I ask four questions that help me characterize anyone's way of thinking. In various forms and on many occasions, they are "What is the nature of Reality?" "What is a person's highest pursuit?" "What is wrong with the world?" and, "How do you fix it?" Since understanding each world view is foundational to the Conversation, I answer these questions early on, relating each father's perspective.

Like with many philosophies, there is a lot to learn from how a person handles "the big three": Money, Sex, and Power. John and Dad view money differently. They might say that they view it similarly, but their behavior is different, it tells a different story. What can you learn about a person by observing how he handles money or uses power? What can you tell about a person by the way she views sex? In any case, especially with sex, people do not talk about their views very often or with much candor. A person's behavior, however, makes him an open book. Because of my relationship to each man, our secret conversations revealed deep considerations of these issues.

As much as any ideas in our culture, Joy, Hope, Meaning, and Faith have been claimed by Western Christians much more than their secular—and certainly atheist—counterparts. Because Ayn Rand builds her doctrine on "rational self-interest," Reason and Capitalism appear more closely aligned with the atheist intellectual community. However, Rand has much to say about these ideas of Meaning and Faith—and even that which is left unsaid serves to instruct us. (Consider what she does not say about the origins of the universe or when life begins.) For example, Ayn Rand's philosophy is profoundly metaphysical, while not theistic. She is driven by the truths she finds unequivocally objective; and she is by no measure either a nihilist or a relativist. Joy, like Meaning, may find a very different object for the Christian, yet it can be argued that Joy was Ayn Rand's highest pursuit. Whether or not her detractors understand the idea of Selfishness as Rand meant it, they use that term against her with little room for engagement.

While each world view challenges the other, their agreements may surprise you, as they have surprised me. In my life with my fathers, I set out to promote understanding. I pursued this Conversation. As a result, thoughtful people with disparate world views considered another perspective. The cathartic journey was, in retrospect, inevitable. The journey is the story. I could list the areas of opposition and reconciliation, but the journey itself has put the flesh on the bare bones of the intellectual puzzle. Each of the subsequent chapters addresses foundational matters in society. Both Christianity and Rand's philosophy have infused our culture with unavoidable perspectives that the Conversation of this book will illuminate.

Part I

INITIATING CONVERSATION:

THE BEGINNING OF A JOURNEY

I

BACKSTORY

Everyone who meets John immediately likes him. He's charismatic, funny, and anyone can see he's passionate. Ask him about business, and he'll start in on Capitalism and from there move to philosophy. You might never find out about the companies he started and took public. Ask him about living life, and you'll hear about his family, his race horses, and his love of poker. He probably wouldn't volunteer that he won the United States Poker Championship (and "somewhere around a million bucks") in 2004. Because that's just the way he rolls. You'd like John. But, as a young man growing up in his house, I hated his guts.

Dad was bigger than life, and I always felt strong when I walked beside him. Muscular and intense, he actually represented everything good about the word "macho." I had never seen anyone beat him in tennis, racquetball, or swimming. A PhD, genius IQ, quirky, paranoid, and unpredictable, even dangerous. Had we been contemporaries, I probably would not have sought him as a friend. But Dad is fiercely loyal, and I could not have done better.

When John moved in, a lot changed. There were new rules, new ways of doing things, and it was all disorienting. Nothing was familiar. We moved out of the neighborhood where I grew up, to a "nicer" town and started spending more time with John's family. It was strange because, while I was welcomed by this friendly tribe of Italian-Americans, I knew no one could possibly understand my resentment and inner alienation. I felt like I'd "hit bottom;" and I was only eleven.

It is embarrassing to admit, but I was a pathetic misfit in junior high: awkward and a people-pleaser, especially adults. Confidence has never been what I would call my life's theme. It was more than wanting to be liked and included; I was desperate. I kept asking everyone if they wanted to be my friend. Ironically, I had no friends. At the time, I had no idea what drove me to that level of neediness. Looking back, I think it was my parents' divorce. There was always lots of yelling: scary for an eleven-year-old. I needed to be strong for my younger sister, but it was I who crawled into her room to find comfort. Even though they couldn't get along, it crushed me when my mom and dad split up. When they fought, I felt alone and exiled from the world. When they finally separated, I died.

Despite the bulky emotional baggage I carried to contain my resentment toward John, I listened to him. My rational mind couldn't deny that he made sense. I did not admit it, but John taught me more about philosophy than any of my teachers through college *and* graduate school. To this day, I maintain that the kitchen table is a more powerful venue than any classroom. My sister and I used to sit at the dinner table and dread the inevitable continuation of the "lecture series" on whatever topic current events brought to mind; and it was here that Ayn Rand held court. While most families worshipped in church or synagogue, mine worshipped in the pages of *Atlas Shrugged*. John preached eloquently about everything from the depths of Altruism's evil to the zenith of Reason and rationality. At eleven, I wasn't exactly riveted. However, it wasn't his philosophy that fostered my resentment toward John. It was his very existence.

I don't know precisely when Mom and John got married. They never told me. By that time, I had learned not to expect to be included in events like that. It wasn't even a topic that we discussed at the dinner table. What did we discuss?

> *Through many long dinner lectures and monologues, I learned the vocabulary and values of Ayn Rand's Objectivism.*

Philosophy. Through many long dinner lectures and monologues, I learned the vocabulary and values of Ayn Rand's Objectivism. I learned to esteem Reason and objectivity; I learned that ideas have consequences and that everyone cannot be right. I learned the role of government and the joys of Capitalism. I didn't know about Ayn Rand as a person, but her ideas were shaping what would become my personal philosophy. From time to time, I considered the philosophy against the circumstances in which I learned it. It was hard for me to divorce the ideas of Ayn Rand and the man who took my family away, the purveyor of those ideas. I didn't dare give voice to my questions, but they contributed to an inner struggle. And the ongoing debate was painful, like the painful knot you get in your stomach when you receive an unexpected diagnosis. High school would bring some welcome distractions; yet it was also in high school that Objectivism would begin to resonate as a philosophy.

I began high school in a new town, new friends, a new life. I met new people and, relatively speaking, fit in to this new environment. Classes were interesting. I liked school. My grades were good and, for the first time, I discovered the camaraderie of high school athletics. Being a wrestler became my identity. I took everything seriously and the disciplines of wrestling matched the intensity of my temperament. I was good, but I purposely avoided thinking about it. I didn't want to jinx it. I was undefeated on the freshman team, and I got to wrestle some JV matches as well, again undefeated. I had a girlfriend. My life was going well.

My sophomore year brought effortless prosperity: more friends, athletic success, and more opportunities to build my confidence. I was charting my own course, and my prospects were good. I felt like an Objectivist. I was not willing to grant John a place in my heart, but I could embrace Ayn Rand and still hold my stepfather at arm's length. Pursuing my own self-interest in the course of a life well lived, however, something was to catch me off guard. Without warning, I was slammed to the mat, yanked and flipped unexpectedly, like an opponent executing a flawless take-down. "CRACK!"

"My rib!" I moaned, as the emergency room physician entered the exam room, three hours later. "I heard the crack when I hit the wrestling mat."

"*That* must have hurt!" the doctor responded. He looked at the x-ray that revealed a broken rib.

"Not so bad," I said, wanting to be the tough guy.

The doctor joked, "Well, good news! I think you're going to live." As he looked at the x-ray more closely it became apparent there was more. "There's a shadow on the x-ray that... We'd better do some more tests just to be sure." I thought to myself, "I'm fine."

The tests led to biopsies, and those results demanded more tests. Succeeding weeks were filled with doctor visits. There was poking and prodding and extended hospital stays...and then came the day: a kind of before and after moment that you can't see coming, and you only realize in hindsight.

"I'm going to use the word 'cancer,' but I don't want that to scare you." The doctor was nothing if not a straight shooter. "It's just a word that means 'growth,'" he said. "You have a malignant tumor in between your lungs and we think the cancer has spread throughout your upper body." My mind went numb and I felt myself observing the scene from a place above the examination table.

"I'm sorry... What?" I didn't know what to say. "But, I'm sixteen. I don't have cancer. Sixteen-year-olds don't even get cancer... Wait a minute. What did you just say?" It took a while to sink in. I could not have known that everything I had learned in the last sixteen years of life was about to be put on trial.

I spent the next several weeks in the hospital. When I returned home, I started daily radiation treatments. They called it "therapy" but that sounds more like a spa than a hospital ward that literally smelled of burnt flesh. As if the smell didn't make me nauseous enough, the radiation accumulated in my body until I couldn't get up off the bathroom floor. I vomited in the morning before I went to school. Sometimes I was okay till noon, but I couldn't eat. As long as I sat still, classes took my mind off the lightheadedness. After a day of stares, confusion, and pity from my peers, I went for treatment. I'm sure Mom took me most of the time, but what remains with me are the days I went alone: from the school to the train, to the bus, to the hospital. I wanted to ask her to drive me, but it wasn't always easy for me.

Growing up, I learned that emotions are unnecessary at best, and uncomfortable and unmanageable at worst. When my parents fought, it was terrifying to me. These people who were responsible for me—the ones who kept me safe and took care of me—were fighting. As they were pushing each other away (sometimes literally), they were breaking me apart emotionally. Emotions, I learned, are dangerous. They must be contained.

Within a year of my parents' divorce, my father moved to Missouri. I lived in New Jersey with my mother, sister, and stepfather; and my father lived 1,500 miles away. It was set up so that we would go stay with him for extended times on vacation and in the summer. As I spent time with either of my parents, I saw how each responded when I mentioned the other, and it wasn't always pleasant, so I learned to hide my feelings. I learned to manage my parents' emotions by withholding my own. I also hid other parts of my life. At the depths of my cancer treatments, I retreated deeper into myself. I denied my struggles on the outside, but I couldn't contain myself when I was alone. I remember being angry and screaming into my pillow. Frustrated and alone, I would often cry myself to sleep.

I wouldn't have dared ask about the reason for my pain or anyone else's. I wanted to be rational. Instead, I practiced a different mode of survival: denial. It wasn't rational to avoid dealing with Reality, but I constantly denied the seriousness of my condition, much to the dismay of the adults who were shocked and full of pity when they saw me. Not my family, of course. With them, there was no discussion. By going the road of business-as-usual, we could confine the emotional waterfall to a slight dripping: annoying but manageable. I never really felt like I could talk about it.

I had a bad dream as a little kid, after watching a scary movie. In my nightmare, all of the people in my life—my mom, grandparents, sister, even Dad—were replaced by robots, and they were coming to get me! Strangely, the "dad" robot actually looked out for me, tried to help me escape the other robots. And now, as a teenager in the slow recovery from cancer, I missed him. His absence made me feel even more isolated. I didn't want to make him feel guilty, so I couldn't tell him the pain I was going through. In the mass of medical issues that I couldn't manage, at least I could manage to keep the baggage out of my parents' way. I was never good at cleaning my room, and the mess used to frustrate and exhaust my parents. Maybe now, I could tidy up my life and avoid the unsightly mess of my emotions.

I wanted to please my parents, especially Dad. That's probably why, even while living with my atheist mother and stepfather, I started going to church. Of course, Dad wasn't around, but I'm sure I told him. The son of a Presbyterian minister, this was something he could understand. Still, it was strange because I wasn't a very likely churchgoer. Church was like comfort food: not a lot of food value, but I felt better when I ate it. The rest of my family stayed home, as I walked the honorable mile to worship. It was in those formative youth groups and Sunday sermons that my theological conundrums began to challenge my philosophical leanings. Like many of the churches I have attended, there were people with painfully rigid postures who seemed determined to avoid laugh lines. And there were others, like Stuart, a young seminary student, whose face was more weathered, but less bothered. Stu was willing to listen. His compassion and understanding kept me coming back. I was somewhere between those two types, not stiff like the first, but more confined and less free than Stu. I still felt alone, but hopeful.

Dad was a loner at his core. Undoubtedly his fierce intellect and difficulty with people contributed to this. His aloneness always resonated with me. Maybe that's why I identified with him so much more than the other adults in my life. Still, it felt threatening to talk about the deepest concerns of my heart. Instead of talking with anyone, I held it in. From time to time during my radiation treatments, I found myself feeling utterly alone. My family downstairs watching television and me upstairs vomiting and screaming into my pillow, not so loud that anyone would hear. "Why me?" I begged someone to answer. "Why is this happening? What did I do to deserve this?" I wailed to the point of exhaustion, or until I found the perfect position on my bedroom floor or in the bathroom, whatever would keep the balance and forestall the heaving convulsions. I didn't want to move, or breathe.

"Hold your breath. Don't breathe." The radiology technician recited these words over the intercom in a singsong every few minutes. Her sterile voice complemented the fluorescent lights and the fetid smell of the radiology department. The treatments themselves were painless enough, but I knew what was coming.

Every day stepped up the level of sickness, the intensity accumulating throughout the week and starting over again on Monday. By Friday, I was a mess. It was challenging to go to school, but it provided some distraction. The real work began after school, as I headed to the hospital for my final treatment for the week. Taking the train from the suburbs—what I later understood to be the "reverse commute"—was usually uneventful. As I boarded the city bus, the first few whiffs of dread approached. The bus stopped just two blocks from the hospital, and I learned exactly how to navigate the university hospital maze. Once I reached the waiting room and checked in, it wasn't usually a long wait. I was actually better off when the wait was long because I hated going into the treatment room. It was like being taken from purgatory. My nostrils had been branded by the smell of flesh, being burned by the radiation and the pungency of bodies refraining from lotions or deodorants for medical reasons.

I especially hated it when my mom took me in. I felt like I had to manage her emotions. Like she was doing this for me and I had to keep her company or somehow entertain her so it would be worth her effort. She would be mortified if she knew that I was thinking this way: all the more reason to avoid the occasion.

I jumped up when my name was called. The drill had become second nature. Less than an hour later, I was out of there. The bus that took me back stopped across the street. The body odor and bus fumes were no worse on the ride home, but this time there were more people. I was less likely to get a seat, even as a frail youth with pasty, near-translucent skin and patches of hair missing. By the time I reached the train, I was somewhat dizzy. By the end of the train ride, I usually couldn't contain myself any longer. I shuffled off the platform with the commuters, and my nausea gripped me. As people dispersed through the parking lot, I found a spot next to the curb on the suburban sidewalk, and threw up. That describes most of the days of my sixteenth year.

By the time my course of radiation reached completion, it was the end of a long winter that had stretched into a year. During the spring and summer, my hair started growing back. My body—weak from weeks of vomiting, dehydration, and weight loss—began to regain fifty pounds of flesh and muscle. My skin was no longer a translucent blue. My health started to recover.

Summer finally came. My treatments were officially over, at least for a time. The only thing I wanted to do was get out. I hadn't seen Dad since my surgery, months ago, and it didn't take me long to see that he had undergone some major changes. He was the same person, but there was actually more of him. Not physically more; he'd never been in better shape. But it wasn't really his personality either. It was like all of the positive aspects of his character had overcome the negative ones. Dad had this phrase that he used to say when he wanted my sister and me to stop fighting or otherwise be on our best behavior. He would say, "Tennis court manners." That's because Dad was a different person when he was on the tennis court. I dated a girl whose father took tennis lessons from Dad and he described him as "the nicest guy I've ever met." When I heard that, I thought, "Dad? Do you even know the person you're talking about?" That was the guy that I was seeing for the first time, now in real life, off the tennis court. It wasn't a charade or something temporary; he was truly different. Where was the rage, superiority, condescension, and militant need to be right? He never talked about it, but it had been superseded by patience, understanding, and a hint of wisdom that had been in the background before. Looking back, it could have been me. Maybe I had changed and was noticing Dad from a new perspective. If it weren't for some more concrete examples, I would have left it there. But there were some things that didn't compute. Dad, ever the loner and introvert, started opening up to others through a new church group. One morning I awoke to the strangest sight I had ever seen. Dad and his wife, Debbie, were kneeling on the living room floor, praying.

I had heard stories, but I had never been exposed to someone who took his Christian Faith so seriously. Until this time, most of my images of Christians were in the context of polite tea and cookies in Fellowship Hall or the austere religion of my grandmother. She was a retired school teacher and ran a very tight household, so I played outside a lot. She tied her long, gray hair in a bun at the back of her head and always wore an expression that indicated sternness and detachment from the silliness around her. She gave me the idea that Christianity was about moral austerity and volunteerism. From her, I learned all of the things that I was too lazy to do, but should be doing. She helped me build the conviction that the things you most want to do are always unattainable. Her look inflicted certain guilt, even if I didn't know what I had done or left undone. She made me feel ashamed sometimes, but I knew she loved me. I wanted to be around her because she was strong and got things done. She was kind-hearted and always worked hard. Heaven, as I understood it, was full of people like my grandmother, who had lived actively good lives and suffered without enjoyment in order to earn a place with God. That made logical sense to me.

I had heard stories, but I had never been exposed to someone who took his Christian Faith so seriously.

But seeing Dad's Christian life, and hearing how he talked about Jesus, was unfamiliar if not a little creepy.

I wasn't able to take Dad's experience at face value. We talked, and I asked a lot of questions about his new experiences. At first, I think he was oddly reticent to talk about his new faith, like he was trying to hide something. But I went to church with him anyway. At first, everything seemed weird. Churches come in a wide variety of flavors and colors, but they basically all look and feel the same from the outside. Beneath the building and the décor, it's the people who differentiate. Dad described it differently. He seemed to think there was something supernatural going on in the lives of the people he encountered.

That summer, I began wrestling with ideas. Not the same ideas I explored with John at the kitchen table. Objectivism was an intellectual exercise for me, and Ayn Rand helped me cope. Now I began looking for specific answers to real-life problems: mere coping was no longer enough. How do I respond to suffering and pain? What matters in the realm of human relationships? How do I overcome my own fears and weaknesses so that I won't be shut down by them? What is the meaning behind my life, the painful parts and the times that are full of joy? Is my life worth anything in the scheme of things?

Ideas that were clear at the dinner table became fuzzy in the outside world. Through Ayn Rand, John taught that my convictions have consequences in every area of my life. What I believe about how the universe is put together affects whether I will study for my next exam. What I believe is wrong with the world influences the way I feel when I read the *Financial Times* in the morning. How I think the world should be fixed impacts the decision I make to accept that job offer—or keep looking. I see now that a person's world view is the sum of many experiences, and parental impact can dwarf all of these life experiences combined.

That's especially true for the influence of a father. In my case, I had two father figures, with two vastly different views of the world. I think that's why I've struggled with my world view. To this day, I haven't reached full resolution to the conflict between the two.

My extraverted temperament has influenced the way I approach reconciling my two father figures and their world views. I process things out loud, and the discussion gives me clarity. I don't know all the answers, but I think I'm looking in the right place. Something like a Conversation has played out in my mind over the last thirty years, and it continues to become more nuanced with every book, essay, and discussion. And that's how I've approached this

> *In my case, I had two father figures, with two vastly different views of the world.*

book. When I asked questions as a sixteen-year-old, I got sixteen-year-old answers. As an adult, answers that were satisfying to that teenager are no longer sufficient. The ensuing restlessness has led me to Ayn Rand's writing over and over again for fresh perspective, digging deeper with each decade. I read a lot that provides "the other side" or "equal time" among Christian apologists, but most of the apologies address the more prevalent post-modern mentality that stems from the relativism of my college days at Brown. Through graduate school, it was hard to get Ayn Rand's ideas on the same page as the philosophers and intellectuals who hold the Gospel so close. I've struggled personally, and the Conversation of my life keeps returning to my relationships with these two men. While the Conversation is challenging on an intellectual and emotional level, the spiritual dimension has been the trickiest.

"The soul of what?!?" my friend Cathy said when she read a posting on my Facebook page. "Atlas," I said, like I knew she was teasing. "It's the title." Ayn Rand's "Atlas" represents the prime movers of society, the producers of the world, achievers, the creators of value. I continued, "When they shrug, it's not as if they don't care anymore. They're heaving the load of the world from their backs and going on strike." I explained that I had started to frame my world view around Ayn Rand's philosophy until my spiritual crisis provoked questions that Objectivism didn't even recognize as valid.

"What do you mean?" John objected. "I'm spiritual. I'm more spiritual than any of those so-called religious fundamentalist nutcases out there. Jesus Christ!" I never considered John to be "spiritual," because Ayn Rand looked at spirituality differently than others. John's spirituality didn't consist of something entirely separate from his material body, and he didn't think of his soul as something mystical or supernatural. The spirit of his moral principles ruled his own consciousness. Morality, Reason, Freedom, and rational self-interest—these were the virtues that guided his life, and they should guide mine, too. Not because he said so, but because it is the nature of Man to live by these truths.

Yet, the prospect of something more intrigued me. In spite of Rand's mantra "Wishing doesn't make it so," I wished. My Objectivist family dismissed everything religious long ago, and, on the contrary, none of my Christian friends wanted to talk about Objectivism, even if they *had* heard of Ayn Rand. As far as it depended on me, I was seeking, but I could not have told you for what.

By the time I was in college, I started to digest my confusion and the discord of my life. My experiences accelerated adulthood, but there was hope. Exploring my fathers' world views became my way to reconcile my fathers to the child in me that was left behind. While my intellect had accelerated to adulthood many years before, my emotions had yet to experience puberty. My intellect gave me a platform to engage with these two powerful, life-shaping voices. The Conversation that ensued launched me on a path toward emotional and spiritual reconciliation.

2

TWO VOICES

*T*he *Soul of Atlas* has two heroes; the same two are villains. My fathers are two distinct voices, and I am caught in the middle, like an infant, unaware of the substance, knowing only that discord and loud argument mean something is amiss. It has been my quest to reconcile these opposed perspectives, as I sought to reconcile the men and my relationships with each of them.

As with most stories, you may identify one world view as the protagonist and the other as the antagonist, especially when the two emerge from opposite ends of the philosophical universe. Often, the hero and the villain are obvious. This story unfolds differently: more like a Conversation than a story. Maybe my fathers are neither heroes nor villains. Perhaps the real hero is Truth. The story begins with Truth's identity crisis and follows his quest to find himself. As a protagonist, Truth is hard to dislike. I think I have always wanted Truth, whether or not it was attainable.

Why a World View? Why Two?

My struggle to articulate a coherent view of the world began long before college. From the earliest discussions I can remember, both Dad and John told me it was important to grasp and articulate the way I see the world around me. Everything gets filtered through that fundamental perspective. I was impressionable. More than that, I soaked up everything that my two fathers said to me without pausing to consider the contradictions. I wanted their love, and their approval. For me, the emotional came first. I wanted to understand these two men and their way of seeing the world. Sometime later, the pursuit of a world view became Intellectual. But the emotional longing for John and Dad's approval loomed in the background.

Dad always said it was crucial to know the philosophical underpinnings of my world view. In my foundational, world view-building college days, a visiting philosopher came to campus. Someone messed up the scheduling, so the university had no idea he was coming through on his tour of the Ivy League, and it turned out he was a brilliant thinker and prolific writer. Instead of speaking to a large crowd, he met with a couple students for coffee outside the bookstore. He spoke about world views. It was like he had known me all my life—and my struggle. Interestingly, he held a Christian world view, and I felt like he was channeling Dad. "You need to understand others' philosophies in order to understand your own, fully and deeply. I'm convinced that for a person to be fully conscious intellectually he should not only be able to detect the world views of others but be aware of his own—why it is his and why in the light of so many options he thinks it is true."[1]

John, too, belabored the importance of understanding others' world views, but in a somewhat more combative way. He made it his life's mission to drill Truth into the impressionable heads of my sister and me. Instead of recognizing what he could learn from others, he did reconnaissance. "Understand the enemy." It was like he was constantly reciting Ayn Rand's essays. In *Philosophy: Who Needs It*, Rand included her speech to West Point's graduating class.

> *In your own profession, in military science, you know the importance of keeping track of the enemy's weapons, strategy and tactics—and of being prepared to counter them. The same is true in philosophy: you have to understand the enemy's ideas and be prepared to refute them; you have to know his basic arguments and be able to blast them.* [2]

Without knowing it, I combined Dad and John's approaches. With the Objectivist and Christian world views, I became a detective and a military strategist. I was a double, triple, quadruple agent—going to and from the enemy camp—never quite knowing friend from foe. After a while, the confusion compounded.

The Soul of the Fathers

Reconciliation. I longed for it, but there was never so much as a common understanding between my two father figures. Each thought he understood the other, but I knew they were miles apart. More tragically, I was on the other side... from every vantage point. I was always opposed, in some way, to the perspective of the father figure in front of me. Ironically, I was desperate for their approval. I couldn't help myself.

In the process of seeking reconciliation, I became the pivot point of this Conversation. I was in the eye of the storm. Instead of a calm perspective on the tempestuous winds, I was whipped in opposite directions: from one world view to the other. The whole time, I was determined to understand each of my fathers, to participate in his world. I became immersed in how they thought. When I spent time with John, I thought like an Objectivist. At the kitchen table, I answered John's instructional questions, and asked him my own, to help me enter into his way of seeing. I listened to Dad as we worked on the farm together. I handed him tools, and he handed me Christian doctrine. I questioned a lot, and categorized the answers over time. Sometimes our discussions were long and disjointed. Often, they were brief and topical. What I learned allowed me to understand the essence of each world view, as if I were staring intently into a soul. Every breakthrough brought me closer to seeing the soul of my fathers.

Four questions helped me understand and compare each world view: What is the nature of the universe? What is an individual's highest pursuit? What is wrong with the world? How do you fix it? Even as I recount them, my experiences with Dad and John afforded many opportunities to think, compare, and search.

The Soul of Reality

What is truly real? What is Reality? A basic question, yet so contentious and hotly debated: a question too lofty to resolve and too practical to ignore. What is the nature of the universe? "It just is," John would say. "I'm not saying that it's not possible that there is some kind of design involved. But there is no reason to believe it's all about chance or probability either. If I ever have to stand before a god—your god, or any god of any kind—I'm just going to say, 'Hey, you didn't give me enough reasonable evidence to make a rational conclusion about your existence.' So, I think I'm okay." He shrugs. John's mannerisms are casual, hiding a subtle shrewdness. He reads people. He reads me like a book. Without showing it, he knows I am hanging on every word. "Let's put it this way: I have a good case. So, I'm comfortable with my situation." For John, the universe is fundamentally impersonal. Man lives by Reason, so Faith is irrelevant.

"But how do you say that the universe came into being?" I asked. How can you say, 'It's just here'?"

"Reality. That's the simple answer to your question, 'What is the nature of the universe?'" John always starts with something provocative. He knows I will pursue it, not let it drop. He says Truth is objective and existence exists apart from how I perceive it.

> *For John, the universe is fundamentally impersonal. Man lives by Reason, so Faith is irrelevant.*

Metaphysically speaking, my father could not be further from John. Dad's universe is designed by a Person. At its soul, the universe is highly personal. Yes, Man lives by Reason, but there is more, and God is real. I raise this objection with John. "But, how did the universe get here, and what is the meaning behind it?" I ask.

"Who knows? It just is. Not to say that there is no meaning to it, I just don't have any evidence about what that is, except what I observe and Reason." There is no evidence in John's Objectivist world to believe that we came about through a Creator, or any other Intelligent Designer. "Maybe we got here by chance; I don't know." Leonard Peikoff said, "The universe is all that exists and all that has ever existed." It's important to note that Ayn Rand did not write about the origins of the universe. She viewed hers as a philosophy "for living on earth." She crafted her understanding of the universe without God at the center. She reasoned, "existence exists," without the need for God and certainly without the need for a Person who creates and sustains the world we live in.

For the forty years I have known him, John has described himself as an atheist, not an agnostic. "The question about God's existence is not open for discussion. We don't need God to explain the origins of the universe.

Let's move on with our lives and not concern ourselves with what is at least an irrelevant waste of time, and unnecessary at best! What I do know," he says, "is my own life. I can observe Reality through my five senses. I have the capacity to reason, to take what I know and organize it into concepts and categories so I can survive and thrive. To that end, I can create value." In John's world view, there is no need and no room for Faith. Ayn Rand wrote this to an inquiring reader:

> *I regret I have even less sympathy or interest than you have in anything relating to the mystical, to the "other-dimensional," the irrational or "super-rational." (I don't believe there are any such things or realms.) I am an atheist. Therefore, I cannot follow you at all if your definition of why the existence of a finite world presupposes that it was created by God. It doesn't.[3]*

Dad's understanding of the universe was totally different. He said, "At the center of the universe is an omnipotent Designer who created and sustains everything."

"That just seems so arbitrary," I said.

Dad startled me. "Arbitrary!" he said, "is exactly what it's not." His voice trailed off. "The order in the universe was designed by an Intelligent Designer, as opposed to chance."

I knew about Aquinas. At least, I studied the cosmological or "First Cause" argument for God, among others. Since everything was caused by something else, it stands that the universe was caused by something, so the universe itself requires a first cause. That's God. But it seemed simplistic. "If everything in the universe requires a cause, why is 'God' an exception?" I asked.

"That's why He's God."

"If you're making an exception for God, why does the series of effects and causes stop there? Why couldn't it stop earlier in the regression, with the appearance of the universe itself?" He admitted that he didn't have an answer.

"I suppose you could stop there, but that doesn't close the case. My understanding of origins needs to be consistent with what I observe today, both philosophically and scientifically. My world view integrates my Reason and experience, especially as they relate to the historical Jesus."

He wasn't really changing the subject, although it seemed like it. He went on to talk about the importance of Jesus's identity: that he is who he says he is, and that he rose from the grave. For Dad, it all hinges on the resurrection. If Jesus overcame death, the game changes altogether. If not, well… I think my father would pack it in.

"The Christian God is personal," he said, "and He created us in His image. Throughout history, God has reached out to us, but we have refused to respond." Dad sees everything in the universe under its Creator. The universe derives its worth, purpose, existence, and nature from God, the Creator and Sustainer of the universe.

He explained to me like this, "The nature of the universe is primarily personal because it originates in the personhood of God." I knew Christian metaphysics stated that God is Reality. To the Christian, he is the ultimate Reality. But Dad expounded, emphasizing that we know what we know about Reality through Reason and experience *because* God created an ordered universe. He created Man in his image with the capacity to reason. It was no surprise to me that Dad put a premium on Reason, although I may not have understood how it so particularly reflected his God.

He continued, "It's true that Man's mind is his means of survival. Because the universe is primarily personal, we cannot know everything through impersonal means."

Ayn Rand's universe, on the other hand, is predominantly impersonal. Emotions exist, but they need to be harnessed to serve the higher faculty of the individual's reason. Personal relationships serve the same purpose: to celebrate the heroic creation of value that sustains and enhances the life of the individual. On a cosmic scale, the Objectivist sees an impersonal world.

Not until Dad explained the Biblical perspective, did I truly grasp the implications of a personal versus impersonal universe. "Relationship," he said, "is at the heart of the universe, by design. Personal relationships aren't a matter of critical observation and Reason, at least not exclusively."

I should point out that Dad's doctoral degree is in exercise physiology. In his study of the sciences, he observed phenomena and reasoned to conclusions. Ayn Rand did the same. But personal relationships go beyond mere observation. "You can learn a lot about the world through observation," Dad said. "But to go beyond that, you need to start thinking about revelation."

In any context, the word "revelation" sounded churchy and mystical, something I would tend to avoid. I thought I knew where he was going with this. It surprised me the first time, but I have heard it more than one time since then.

Dad used different illustrations, but they generally began with getting to know another person. "When you want to get to know a girl," he used to say, "she has to be willing to let you, to reveal something of herself. You can learn a lot by observing, but there comes a point when she controls how much you get. The degree to which you know her depends on what she reveals. If Reality is primarily personal, then a one-page fact sheet won't cut it." In other words, the personal—with its relational vulnerabilities and its dependence on *revelation* as a means to knowledge—is primary. The impersonal is necessary, but it only goes so far. Our need for one another—for relationship—derives from our need for God. That made sense to me.

The Soul of Humanity

Pride is the recognition of the fact that you are your own highest value and, like all of man's values, it has to be earned.[4]

— Ayn Rand

The "soul" of humanity refers to Man's highest purpose: the essence of what it means to be human. Not to be confused with "the human soul," it is the highest possible occupation of an individual's mind, will, and emotions. If you could identify one thing that makes life worth living, what would that be?

John didn't miss a beat. "It's my own life. That's the meaning of life: to survive. And not only that, to thrive. Happiness in this life (because there is no other) is the end purpose. There is nothing more, no cosmic meaning beyond the obvious. Of course, without my life, I would have no values, so my life is the Ultimate Value. Nothing else matters." Rand said that an individual's life is the standard of value.

> *There is only one fundamental alternative in the universe: existence or nonexistence—and it pertains to a single class of entities: to living organisms.*[5]
>
> — John Galt

Shakespeare presaged Rand in his character's immortal contemplation, "To be or not to be." Unlike Hamlet, Ayn Rand makes no hesitation in her answer. Her alternative to existence in our conscious state is unconsciousness. Therefore, for anything living, its life is its fundamental value, since existence or nonexistence is its fundamental alternative. Any organism has to exist according to its means of survival. Humans live by the exercise of the mind—Reason—because Man is a rational being. These were the basics of Rand's thoughts that were drummed into me from adolescence. John explained things with his characteristic passion.

"The purpose of morality converges on one goal: the life of the individual and whatever will perpetuate and enhance it. And that's how Ayn Rand defines morality. Whatever contributes to the highest possible value—the life of the individual—is a virtue."

"So, if that's virtue," I asked, with only a hint of teenage snideness, "what's the vice?"

The answer was obvious. "Anything that degrades or diminishes the individual's life is a vice; and that's why Ayn Rand lives in a world where there are moral absolutes without a moral absolute giver. Do you see how straightforward her reasoning is? From the ultimate value of the individual's life, Rand reasons to moral absolutes. She does not appeal to a greater authority than her own Reason. She does not require Faith in a Higher Power, and she certainly rejects any subjectivity in determining these absolutes." John was more than pleased with the answer. It was his bedrock philosophy.

From him I learned that commitment to rational values actually led to happiness. John always talked about Rand's definition of true happiness. He paraphrased it often: "True happiness is a state of non-contradictory joy and it's available to those who pursue rational values."

In Aristotle's estimation, happiness is the result of a life lived well. Accordingly, there is one right plan for the good life. Pleasure (not pain), satisfaction (not dissatisfaction), and all of the obvious things that contribute to happiness in life require, first and foremost, a life. Rand concludes, with Aristotle, that one's very life is the standard of value. Surviving is a means to "living well," and "living well" is an end in itself. The "good life" is the right ultimate end that we all should seek. Unquestionably, I had seen John exemplify this. And while Aristotle concedes that the "good life" may work out differently for everyone, Rand takes it a step further.

If the soul is the essence of something, the soul of John Galt is captured in the utterance of these words: "I swear by my life and my love of it that I will never live for the sake of another man nor ask another man to live for mine."[6] He pursues that which will sustain and enhance his own life. Rand makes it clear that every man is an end in himself, not a means to the ends of others; he must live for his own sake, neither sacrificing himself to others nor sacrificing others to himself. He must work for his own rational self-interest, with the achievement of his own happiness as his highest moral purpose.

Christianity, on the other hand, seemed less relevant. Pursuing happiness fell outside the domain of Christian endeavor. When I challenged Dad on that count, he referred me to Pascal. Blaise Pascal asserts that, without exception, all men seek happiness.

> *Whatever different means they employ, they all tend to this end. The cause of some going to war, and of others avoiding it, is the same desire for both, attended with different views. The will never takes the least step but this object. This is the motive of every action of every man, even of those who hang themselves.*[7]

Furthering Pascal's observations, John Piper writes, "As far as he was concerned, seeking one's own happiness… is a simple given of human nature. It is a law of the human heart as gravity is a law of nature."[8] Rand, in fact, rails on Kant and the Stoics for their condemnation of self-interest. She rightly condemns the exaltation of self-denial as an end in itself: the idea that it is a virtue to "go without" period, full stop. And, unlike some evidence to the contrary, self-denial for its own sake is simply not a part of the Christian Faith. In *The Weight of Glory*, C. S. Lewis continued this line of thinking.

> *If we consider the unblushing promises of reward and the staggering nature of the rewards promised in the Gospels, it would seem that Our Lord finds our desires not too strong, but too weak. We are half-hearted creatures, fooling about with drink and sex and ambition when infinite joy is offered us, like an ignorant child who wants to go on making mud pies in a slum because he cannot imagine what is meant by the offer of a holiday at the sea. We are far too easily pleased.*[9]

I agree with Lewis that human beings do not seek their own happiness with a fraction of the resolve and passion they should. I think Ayn Rand would agree, too. They satisfy their appetite with mud pies instead of infinite delight. Of course, she stops far short of praising God as an object of worship. We worship what is supremely valuable to us, and Rand's object of worship is the individual. There are some things that are so valuable to us that they are indispensable to who we are; they "shape our worth." By definition, these are what we worship. In the words of Bob Dylan, "You've gotta' serve somebody." In our pursuit of happiness or fulfillment (I equate the two) the Objectivist and the Christian look in different places, but they are seeking an answer to the same question. Put another way, everyone's worth is shaped by something, and that is what we serve. This is the endeavor of Man's highest purpose, be it his own life or glorifying God.

Asked the question, John and Dad each says that he holds the higher view of humanity. Both Objectivism and Christianity, unlike Pantheism and many other world views, elevate humanity above the level of any other living being. John believes that Man is unique because of his capacity to reason, his cognitive ability. Dad believes that Man is created in the image of God, unlike any other aspect of God's creation. As a consequence, Man can reason, choose, and orient his life to experience God and glorify the One who made him.

In Dad's view, God is the Ultimate: not only the Ultimate Reality, but also humanity's highest occupation. "He makes values possible, objectively, not dependent on one person's cultural, ethnic, or economic perspective. God is Ultimate, and anything less than God is an idol, like the idols in the Old Testament that the people of God worshipped and served instead of the Living God."

What is the difference between what John serves and what Dad serves? It's not enough to say that an Objectivist pursues his own self-interests, because we've already said that our own happiness or self-interest is a simple given in human nature. Our pursuit of that happiness depends on how we view the world. John and Dad view the world differently. So, how does John pursue happiness differently than Dad? John focuses on producing, creating, making value as the primary, most basic function of Man. It is in the nature of Man to create value by using his mind.

> *It matters not how strait the gate,*
> *How charged with punishments the scroll.*
> *I am the master of my fate:*
> *I am the captain of my soul.*[10]
>
> —William Ernest Henley, *Invictus*

As a prime mover, he values producing, creating value, over everything else. His worth derives from his ability to produce. Without producing, he is not fulfilling what it is in his nature to do. What decides the Objectivist's worth? The value he creates: the buildings that stand, the bridges that hold, the trains that deliver. If his productions fail, he is devalued. If his buildings fall; if his bridges do not hold; if his trains do not run; if he does not produce, he cannot fulfill his own conception of value. He is worthless.

The Christian does not see his value in what he can do, but in something less transient, less temporal. The verdict on his worth does not depend on his work; it depends on God. Furthermore, the very Object that decides the Christian's worth is what provides his happiness. The Psalmist sees that these have the same Source.

> *Then will I go unto the altar of God, unto God my exceeding*
> *joy: yea, upon the harp will I praise thee, O God my God.*
>
> — Psalm 43:4 (KJV)

> *In thy presence is fullness of joy; in thy right hand there are*
> *pleasures forever.*
>
> — Psalm 16:11 (KJV)

Dad measures value without reference to what he can produce. That does not mean he does not value production. He produces, but neither his production, nor his capacity to produce is the measure of his worth as a person. And that includes what he might achieve for God.

God is not a means to some other pleasures. God is the ultimate end of the search. In Piper's words, Christianity "does not reduce God to a key that unlocks a treasure chest of gold and silver. Rather it seeks to transform the heart so that 'the Almighty will be your gold and choice silver to you.'"[11]

Not everything that the Christian existentialist, Søren Kierkegaard, said makes sense to me, but what he said about sin has bolstered my understanding of what Christians call "the Gospel." He said that sin is finding your identity in anything other than God. And the positive corollary to that can be found, among other places, in the Westminster Shorter Catechism: The chief end of Man is to glorify God and to enjoy Him forever. There are several points in that statement and more adept minds than mine have expounded on them over the centuries. Yet the core of the statement asserts that the highest possible occupation for the Christian is God himself, what is called "his Glory." Indeed, for the Christian, this is the answer to the question of humanity's highest purpose.

The Soul of the Problem

I honestly wouldn't characterize either of my fathers as a whiner, but it seemed that I was always hearing about the world's problems. Watching politicians defend their actions on Sunday morning talk shows offered John one of his favorite platforms for expounding on the essence of what is wrong with the world today. There was plenty of armchair quarterbacking, even though our home was a football-free zone. Instead of the big game, our NFL showdowns were the economy, the culture, and especially the government. The party affiliation mattered a lot less than the approach to the issues. John's rants were by no means random. There was always a pattern, a theme, to describe what was wrong with the world, and it lined up with Ayn Rand's contention, namely that the ills of the world could be traced back to bad philosophy. And bad philosophy leads to bad morality and bad behavior.

In her journals, Rand wrote, "The thing most wrong with the world [is] lack of all values."

> *The lack of principle in capitalism drives men to communism as the cure. Precisely the opposite is true. The evil is not too much selfishness, but not enough of it; not lack of collectivism, but too much of it. The cure—not the destruction of individualism, but the creation of it. Christianity as the hatred of all ideals.[12]*

John said, "The world is full of bad philosophy, bad ideas about the way the world works. Ideas have consequences, you know." Because of the bad philosophy we enter into, we settle for something less than what sustains and embraces us, something less than what is truly satisfying.

> *Dagny, the whole world's in a terrible state right now. I don't know what's wrong with it, but something's very wrong.[13]*
> — Dan Conway, president of Phoenix-Durango railroad

Dan Conway is one of *Atlas Shrugged's* minor heroes. In this quote, he addresses Dagny Taggart, perhaps the most dynamic heroine in modern literature, and Rand's Ideal Woman. As she sees industrialists like Dan Conway losing their will to fight, she is infuriated. The looters are making him a victim of their bad philosophy by violating his individual rights.

> *Whatever else they may disagree about, today's moralists agree that ethics is a subjective issue and that the three things barred from its field are: reason—mind—reality.*

If you wonder why the world is now collapsing to a lower and ever lower rung of hell, this is the reason.[14]

Atlas Shrugged describes a world where train wrecks, market collapses, industrial destruction, and failing business empires are tied inextricably to such philosophy.[15] Far from an irrelevant discipline relegated to the ivory tower of academia, philosophy is at the heart of the world's predicament. Bad philosophy leads to the violation of an individual's right to life, liberty, and the pursuit of happiness. Bad morality follows. The morality embodied by the producers in *Atlas Shrugged* sets itself against the prevailing morality of the world. The producers are motivated by positive values—life, happiness, achievement. They exalt an individual's ability to create value, which increases their enjoyment of life. Their exploiters are motivated by negatives—death, misery, destruction. Instead of creating value to sustain themselves, they focus on taking value produced by others and distributing it.

Moreover, Rand places any faith-based world view in this category, and Christianity is at the top of her list for several reasons. There is not enough tolerance—let alone adulation and celebration—for the men and women of the mind, the only ones creating value, wealth, and well-being.

Did you wonder what is wrong with the world?[16]

— John Galt

John Galt is Ayn Rand's supreme example of a "man of the mind." Well into the story of *Atlas Shrugged*, Galt, announces a strike of the mind. He equates two groups of individuals: the mystics of muscle and the mystics of spirit. The former are those who force production from the men and women of the mind. The latter exploit with guilt and fear, by relying on a "higher form of knowledge," born in the consciousness, that makes their wishes into absolutes.

Rand does not mince words in her disdain for the religious sensibility.

This departure [from reason] is the disease. Religion [is] the greatest disease of mankind.[17]
Religion is also the first enemy of the ability to think... Faith is the worst curse of mankind; it is the exact antithesis and enemy of thought... I want to be known as the greatest champion of reason and the greatest enemy of religion.[18]

According to Rand, it is not only the religious who are problematic, there are actually two groups that attempt to live in opposition to the Objectivist philosophy: Attila and the Witch Doctor. Rand introduces Attila and the Witch Doctor in *For*

> *I want to be known as the greatest champion of reason and the greatest enemy of religion.*
>
> —*Ayn Rand*

the New Intellectual, but similar examples pervade her fiction. In Rand's view, they cast off objective Reality and, with it, Man's true nature. They live in a manner that is not consistent with Man's nature. They are what's wrong with the world. Ayn Rand calls the purveyors of force looters, thieves, criminals, and "Attila" (as in "the Hun") because they take what is valuable by force. They violate the rights of another, specifically his right to property.

While Attila attempts to accomplish his goals through physical force, the second group manufactures its own "reality" by dreaming up its own morality and thrusting it on the consciousness of others. By claiming the moral high-ground, he gives values to the value-less man of force. Rand calls this second group that attempts to survive against the dictates of Man's nature the "Witch Doctor," the mystic, a meta-physicist of whim.

Rand's non-fiction took me further than my conversations with John or Dad. She demonstrates that both groups antagonize Reality by avoiding the correct epistemological basis of knowledge. They don't understand that humans become aware of what exists through their senses, by observation. They integrate those observations into categories or concepts; and so the process of abstract reasoning begins. Instead, Attila acts on instinct and the Witch Doctor determines his morality through mystic, ethereal means originating in his own consciousness. He is informed by whim: arbitrary revelation.

For Rand, the problems that exist today are always traced to such arbitrary revelation, such bad philosophy: the degree that the world departs from the Morality of Life. According to Rand, death is the only state that satisfies the mystics' desire to escape. They want to avoid the reality of living in a manner that is consistent with Man's nature, because evading the true nature of Reality leads to the inevitable consequences of *living for someone else*. Their own lives are not the standard of value. Poverty, suffering, destruction, and death are the consequences of their moral code—and the real motive of the code. Mystics have defaulted on the responsibility to think, act, and produce; they feel envious hatred toward, and wish to destroy, those who have not defaulted. When their mysticism of Faith fails, they resort to force.

The classic hypocritical mystic is James Taggart, Dagny's brother. He is a hollow suit and the epitome of what is wrong with the world. He doesn't think for himself, and so he doesn't create value as a producer. He is a chaotic blend of physical force, skepticism, and the "wisdom" of the collective. Taggart's character and consequent actions illustrate what is wrong with the world Ayn Rand describes in *Atlas Shrugged*.

James Taggart illustrates that poisonous evil comes in a benign, even attractive, package. To say that James Taggart is "skeptical" makes him sound like the elite intellectual who is too smart to be taken in by a simple, unsophisticated fallacy. That's not really what Ayn Rand is getting at. It is, in fact, just the opposite.

In one scene, we find James and his sister, Dagny, arguing about the worthiness of an innovative new metal. Rearden Metal, an alloy produced by Rearden after ten years of experiments, has yet to book its first order. Dagny wants to use the metal to rebuild the tracks for the most important transportation route she runs. Her brother doesn't trust her assessment because he doesn't recognize Reason as a trustworthy means of knowledge. He can't evaluate the new alloy because, according to him, no individual mind can.

> "But..." said Taggart, "but... but nobody's ever used it before!... The consensus of the best metallurgical authorities," he said, "seems to be highly skeptical about Rearden Metal, contending—" "Drop it, Jim."[19]

Taggart continues his objections, challenging Dagny's reliance on her mind against the authority of public opinion and judgments of self-proclaimed "experts."

> "But who says so?"
> "Jim, I studied engineering in college. When I see things, I see them."
> "What did you see?"
> "Rearden's formula and the tests he showed me."
> "Well, if it were any good, somebody would have used it, and nobody has." He saw the flash of anger, and went on nervously: "How can you know it's good? How can you be sure? How can you decide?"
> "Somebody decides such things, Jim. Who?"[20]

From the very beginning and throughout the novel, Rand creates a character we love to loathe in James Taggart. He is feckless and insipid. He discounts the capabilities of the human mind, and he is incompetent himself. And, he's self-centered, falsely humble, and highly dependent on the approval of others.

For example, James Taggart's skepticism means that he does not recognize the authority of Man's mind to evaluate Rearden's new alloy. Still, someone must make a decision, based on some criteria. In his mind, the "consensus" is the only reliable authority: the Collective. Appealing to the collective wisdom of the masses is his way of avoiding any decision and any liability.

Rand articulates only three choices of how to validate our knowledge. She argues that the only valid choice—the choice consistent with Man's existence and nature—is Reason. Anything else is arbitrary; it has no basis in Reality. Faith, superstition, ideas that issue from Man's consciousness—anything opposed to Reason—will ultimately be useless in sustaining and enhancing the life of the individual. When James Taggart has exhausted every avenue known to him, he resorts to physical force.

What's wrong with the Christian's world?

For both fathers, the description of the world's ills is nuanced. Dad says, "We're alienated from God because of our own choices, and we're stuck."

I would respond, "Why would God do that? Why make us in such a way that we could alienate ourselves from God? How could he love us and give us the opportunity to condemn ourselves?"

Dad sighed, "Look at the big picture." Then he launched in. "The Christian narrative is a story about God's Creation, Man's Rebellion, and God's Redemption of his Creation. There is nothing wrong with Creation, the way God designed everything to be. Furthermore, we haven't fully experienced God's ultimate plan for Creation. In the meantime, most of us reject God and choose life without Him. "You want to know what's wrong with the world? It's this alienation that permeates every aspect of humanity."

The alienation stems from two primary places: God's glory and otherness and humanity's sinfulness. God is holy, separated because of his glaring perfection. Every one of us—all of humanity—is sinful. We don't and can't achieve the perfection that allows us to approach God on His terms.

I noticed a book on Dad's table entitled *What's Wrong With the World?* by G. K. Chesterton. "That's got to be the most presumptuous title I've ever seen. Is he serious? Altogether arrogant," I said. That sparked a discussion about what Christians believe and why.

"Not to say that G. K. Chesterton has definitively nailed the Christian view on the world's ills," he said, "but he struck a chord when his book was published, in 1910." He paused for a moment and rubbed his chin in thought. "I think some of his insights are valid today."

> *"You want to know what's wrong with the world? It's this alienation that permeates every aspect of humanity."*

"Like what?"

"Specifically the initial situation of separation and alienation from our Creator. We just weren't designed to live apart from Him."

At one time or another, Dad has shared two analogies with me that illustrate his reasoning. I call the first one the "Refrigerator," and it goes something like this: A man sets out to buy a refrigerator. The one that he settles on has all the gadgets: separate refrigerator compartments with different temperature settings, automatic freezer defrost, plenty of space and nice layout on the inside, built to last. It even has an electronic inventory using scanning technology. It's expensive, but the top of the line. The only instructions are simple: plug it into an electrical outlet with these specifications. He gets the appliance delivered first thing in the morning. He loads his groceries and recalls the simple instructions: "Plug it in." Then, his thought process goes something like this: "For the obscene amount I paid for this refrigerator, it should be self-sufficient. A sophisticated, well-made machine should operate independently." Acting on his conclusion, he leaves the kitchen and thinks nothing more about it.

It's later. He heads to his refrigerator to prepare a meal and finds that all of his food is spoiled. He files a complaint with the manufacturer, and the customer service representative asks him several questions about his use of the product. He explains his reasoning, about the cost of the refrigerator, its sophistication, and his conclusions about the way things are. The customer service person responds like this, in the most respectful way: "It's true that this is a very sophisticated and valuable appliance. In fact, it's the best we have produced to date. Notwithstanding all the built-in technology, this refrigerator was designed in such a way that it won't work properly unless it's plugged in to the appropriate power source. That is not to say that it's an inferior product in any way; it's simply the way it's designed."

Dad believes that human beings were designed by God to be in a relationship with Him. Outside of a relationship with our Creator, we don't work. It's only in communion with Him that we can fulfill the high-point of our humanity.

Dad's second analogy emphasizes the idea of alienation. He imagines landing on Venus, stepping out of the spacecraft and "breathing in that warm Venusian atmosphere (96.5% carbon dioxide, 3.5% nitrogen)." He smiles. "Immediately, you get that feeling of alienation because you're in an environment that doesn't suit your design. While some aspects of life on earth resonate with our human condition, sometimes we simply can't shake the feeling that there is more to life."

The Soul of the Solution

As with the nature of Reality and humanity's highest pursuit, Dad and John diagnose the world both the same and different. The diagnosis is the same in that both say the world—more specifically individuals in the world—should pursue their own self-interest more fervently, without reservation or hesitation. The treatment for the world's ills takes on a different character.

Both Dad and John have been known to say, "We have to get back to the principles and perspectives that made this country great." When each of them speaks about the "founding fathers," he means something altogether different. John refers to Thomas Jefferson and Thomas Paine and their pursuit of individual freedom, with revolutionary courage, guided by Reason, and good philosophy. "We need to apply reason, good philosophy, pursue your own highest self-interest," he says. Dad thinks of James Madison, Samuel Adams, Roger Sherman, Alexander Hamilton, and Patrick Henry. "Freedom to worship and work. Jesus Christ brings us to God. Through Him, we can know and experience the relationship with God that we were designed for." Both fathers talked at length about what we should do to fix the world.

Rand's Fix

In *Atlas Shrugged*, at the climax of the world crisis, the people tune into their televisions and radios to receive some semblance of comfort and direction from the government. One evening, John Galt interrupts all frequencies of the communication spectrum and overrides the official government broadcast. "This is John Galt speaking." In a dramatic monologue, he offers an explanation for the erosion of civilization and attributes it to the false moral code of Altruism and bad philosophy. In a speech that goes on for sixty pages, Galt offers his philosophy as the antidote to the prevailing world view. He describes a world where Reason is the only method of gaining knowledge and dealing with other men, and where morality is based on the virtue of rational self-interest. He invites men everywhere to cease being victims of a system that fails to value the men and women of the mind because they are motivated by self-interest. He calls for the producers to strike: cease producing that which others take away by force and manipulation.

The world you desired can be won, it exists, it is real, it is possible, it's yours.

But to win it requires your total dedication and a total break with the world of your past, with the doctrine that man is a sacrificial animal who exists for the pleasure of others. Fight for the value of your person. Fight for the virtue of your pride. Fight for the essence of that which is man: for his sovereign rational mind.[21]

— John Galt

In Rand's understanding, the morality of the non-producers counts on the producers to think and produce, while denying them the honor they deserve and the freedom they require. Their strategy is to induce moral guilt in the men of Reason and ability. Rand calls this "the sanction of the victim," when an individual or group disregards the rights of individuals. The individuals of the mind are the producers; they create with their mind through innovation, invention, and initiative.

Galt's solution to the ills of the world is (ironically) "Producers of the world unite!" If the producers stop producing, no sanction remains. If the producers leave, no victim remains. So, the solution is to withdraw the sanction of the victim by withdrawing the producers from a political economy that counts on them to think and produce. The strategy to induce moral guilt in the men of Reason and ability will be rendered useless if the strikers refuse to accept guilt for their ability. Through the strike, Galt persuades men and women of ability to withdraw their talents from the world. Without victims, the bad philosophy collapses like a house built on the sand.

Instead of inhibiting the mind and its productive capacity, exalt the mind and its productive capacity. Rand's ideal is a world where everyone pronounces the oath "I swear—by my life and my love of it—that I will never live for the sake of another man, nor ask another man to live for mine."

God's Handiwork

Objectivism and Christianity both advocate a return to Reality. What they do not agree on is what is real. Dad's answer to the inevitable shortcomings of this world is not something that any one of us or even all of together can rectify. "Alienation from God" has neither an individual nor a collective solution. In other words, it's nothing that we can do on our own.

"Because of that," Dad told me, "God must take the initiative. Human beings fall short in that we've lost the focus of the One Thing." Dad referred to the Psalmist, saying, "One thing I ask of the LORD, this is what I seek: that I may dwell in the house of the LORD all the days of my life, to gaze upon the beauty of the LORD and to seek him in his temple."[22] Instead, we think of any number of things that have taken God's place as the supreme occupation of our souls.

At the heart of every human being, apparently, is that God-shaped void that Pascal talked about in his *Pensèes*. Since, in the Christian view, the fundamental problem with humanity is that we are estranged from our Creator, the solution is to come back. We have to deal with the estrangement somehow.

"*We* have to deal with it!?" My incredulity was rarely masked. "*We* are expected to make up for such a thing?"

Dad's response was steady compared to my outburst. "Well, you're right, that's easier said than done, because, frankly, the estrangement is extreme. The Bible says it's analogous to light and darkness, the living and the dead. There is no intermingling between darkness and light. A corpse can't overcome its deadness to initiate a relationship with a living person."

I was attentive, but now making wisecracks about zombies. Uncharacteristically, or maybe *newly* characteristically, Dad displayed patience and even chuckled. Yet his intensity returned swiftly to describe what I knew to be profoundly significant to him.

"But you see, that's exactly what it's like for us and God. We are estranged from Him because we are spiritually dead and He is a Living Spirit. Just like an inanimate corpse is alienated from all living beings, we are stuck in a terminal state of deadness!"

Without meaning to, he had clenched my forearm as he spoke, pressing his point into me physically with his thick, farmer's hand.

Conclusion

Asking and answering the same questions about Objectivism and Christianity helped me understand my fathers. On some aspects of Reality, they disagree: Natural versus supernatural, impersonal versus personal, and revelation—in addition to Reason—as a means of knowledge. On others, they agree. Truth is objective and absolute right and wrong exist, but each approaches Truth differently. Both value reasoning through the evidence, choosing freely, and pursuing happiness with conviction and passion.

Understanding the fundamentals is a long way from reconciliation; it is, rather, where the struggle begins. Are these world views reconcilable? Am I struggling because these world views are, in fact, irreconcilable? Or is my struggle due to a lack of understanding? At this point in my understanding of each world view, I feel like I can speak the language. Every son wants to communicate with his father. It might even be a need or a compulsion! For John and Dad, I started by speaking the language of their world views. I was desperate to know them, and this seemed to be the only route. Understanding my fathers was the first step to communicating.

It was no small feat to build a foundation for understanding the way my fathers view the world. The heavy lifting of figuring out how their conclusions and convictions affect a life well lived required more pointed examination. How do my fathers view, for example, Money, Sex, and Power? In the thick of everyday living, what difference does a philosophy make? I watched closely, asked, and listened. The questions became more specific, and more personal, as I considered my fathers' lives in light of their beliefs.

Part II

TOPICS OF CONVERSATION:

THE LONG ROAD

3

SEX

A s an eleven-year-old child of divorce in the seventies, it seemed my job was to get on with my life, to forget about the aspects of my world that were disintegrating, and to conceal my displeasure with the parental perpetrators of pain. They let me down, despite their stated concern for my well-being. I hid my feelings from everyone, including myself, and I spared them the messiness that I could not even articulate. I understood some of the ugly reasons for the divorce, but there was much more that I didn't understand.

When Dad picked up my sister and me in his candy-apple-red truck, there were almost always tears. "I'm not going to tell you," he used to say, "until you're older. When you're twenty-five—if you still want to know—I will tell you all of the crap that went down." I believe he would have, too, had I been interested by then. At the time, all I really wanted was to enter into his rage, and hurt, and pain. I wanted to feel with him, in solidarity, all that was tearing him apart. Because the truth was that I did feel it, just differently. My world was torn apart, and I blamed John.

Dad suffered the loss of his wife, his children, his home, and he eventually stepped down as president of the company that he started with John and Mom. One other casualty that I never fully appreciated: John and Dad were best friends. The massacre of that relationship was, for me, the most confusing of all, until I read *Atlas Shrugged*.

Mom has always been Dagny. John has said so for as long as I can remember. In his frequent romantic tributes, he recognized, in her, the most glorious manifestations of what he most valued. When I reflect on John's marriage to my mother, it becomes clearer. In its simplest manifestation, Dad was Rearden to Mom's Dagny. Their love was amazing, seemingly meant to be. Then came John Galt. That was John.

Friends come around, share secret pain and triumph, and stay true. True friends remain. In the long moment of my parents' separation and divorce, the splendor of the friendship between Dad and John was lost. I imagine that splendor when I think of them together. Reconciling their world views is more than an intellectual exercise for me. For their sakes and for mine, I longed to see their emotional reconciliation.

My interest in sex was as much about the confusion precipitated by the philosophy as the lostness that came with my experience.

Viewing their relationship in light of the Randian characters they represented was clarifying for me. Sex, while a vital part of the equation, remained a mystery, however, for at least two reasons. Looking to Rand's perspective for insight, I was confused by her descriptions of sex, packed with Freudian landmines and clouded with repressed drives that surface at the wrong place and the wrong time (in her novels and her life). Along with that, my own experience was warped, because I understood neither the Christian nor the Objectivist perspective on sex.

Nevertheless, I needed to understand. My interest in sex was as much about the confusion precipitated by the philosophy as the lostness that came with my experience. And although I grew up in an era permeated by the sexual, there was no real discussion about sex. Sure, my entertainment culture and peer culture were—and are—obsessed with sex: Who's having sex with whom; when…where…how? But is there ever really much substantive discourse on the Why? I am driven by Why. So, in the investigation of "what difference does a world view make?"—sex was fair game.

Personal Crisis

An hour before midnight, the fog started settling. Against the yellow glow of the street lamps, the Narragansett Bay fog met the wet snow, giving the neighborhood around campus the taste of a cold steam room. I was hot, even though it was late November and I had no coat. I could see my breath. I left the campus lounge in a hurry, embarrassed by my confession. My friend Cindy was a committed Christian, and I told her that I had been sexually active with two women for several months. When the two found out about each other, confusion and guilt overwhelmed me. I added that, a half-hour ago in my room, I took pills to forget, to avoid the overwhelming-ness of it all. The irony: the pills were aspirin, and now I was left with ringing in my ears and a heightened awareness of everything. Cindy heard my story and freaked, which is why she called the campus EMTs, who were now looking for me.

I was scared. Exactly how weak was I anyway to run like this? What did it mean that I felt guilty? Six months ago, I was feeling liberated. Sex was my answer to loneliness, but I found myself lonelier than I had ever been. I thought of my Randian parents. They had no hang-ups about sex.

Interestingly, though, we never actually talked about it. I thought *I* was the one with baggage, but that never came up in discussion, either. And somewhere along my ethical journey, I had adopted a Victorian approach to sex. I had mistakenly equated Victorianism with Christianity. My understanding came from studying Victorian poetry as an undergraduate, and from the way Ayn Rand denounced Christianity. The two characterizations were one and the same: rigid, structured, stoic, cerebral, and proper, with a Kantian admixture of Duty and "blind faith." Into that framework, I fit a constricting and confusing view of sex. Rand describes Victorian morals related to sex and says, quite starkly, "That's Christianity." I believed her. On the subject of sex, the Victorian view and Ayn Rand's Objectivist view left no common ground. So, I rejected what I thought was the Christian view, and I tried to embrace Rand.

The two women that I had been so enamored with were nothing like each other, and I was drawn to them for different reasons. Both were smart and physically attractive. One was intense and driven, daring to try anything. The other was full of melancholy, though she had a great sense of humor and a zest for life. Was I attracted to them because they had what I valued in myself, or because they had what I lacked? Perhaps I was just lonely.

Ayn Rand taught me that passionate living is the soul of success and the hallmark of a magnificent mind. Without passion, little of consequence happens. Passion sparks the chemical factories deep in the brain, lighting the emotional fires that turn us on. I know I have passion because it drives me to love, care, want, need, crave, have to have, suffer, and create. Passion is the force behind the momentum of our lives.

The soul refuses to be harnessed. It knows nothing of Day Timers and deadlines and P&L statements. The soul longs for passion, for freedom, for life[1]

— John Eldredge

I used to think that the affair between Mom and John was all about passion and sex. For the longest time, I didn't see how much it was about philosophy. When I finally connected Ayn Rand's philosophy of sex, love, and attraction with John's action and philosophy, I thought he was just using intellectual smoke and mirrors to justify what he had done. If I had any kind of understanding of sex at that time, it was the traditional Judeo-Christian idea that adultery was wrong, mainly because of the brokenness it leaves behind. I guess I had always pictured marriage and sexual intimacy as two personal things that shouldn't be separated. But I neglected to see things from the Objectivist point of view.

John had ideas about his identity and aspirations about what he would become. Sex is more than a physical act or material capacity. Ayn Rand would say that it's an indication of a person's values. "To a rational man," she says, sex is an expression of self-esteem—a celebration of himself and of existence. To the man who lacks self-esteem, sex is an attempt to fake it, to acquire its momentary illusion."[2] John wasn't some sex-starved dog that wandered into my parents' bedroom; he had a family of his own at the time. He wasn't driven by animal passions; he was driven by philosophy. In my mother, he saw "the one."

He met Mom in a community theater production. She was bright, full of action, and passionate about life. It didn't happen overnight, but over time, he was captivated. John's morality was

> *"To a rational man," she says, sex is an expression of self-esteem—a celebration of himself and of existence. To the man who lacks self-esteem, sex is an attempt to fake it, to acquire its momentary illusion."*
>
> *— Ayn Rand*

evolving. He recognized, in her, an intellectual and spiritual equal. In the early days of building their company, he brought skills to the table that Dad didn't have. He was flashy. She admired him for his people skills, his sense of humor, and his ability to get things done. They were both fabulously ambitious, and they worked hard. By comparison, John's other home lacked vibrancy. He made his choice to pursue my mother based on which life fit his view of himself and the story he wanted to fit into. The decision was obvious.

> Romantic love [is man's] response to his own highest values in the person of another—an integrated response of mind and body, of love and sexual desire. Such a man (or woman) is incapable of experiencing a sexual desire divorced from spiritual values.[3]
> ...a man's sexual choice is the result and the sum of his fundamental convictions.[4]

When I first read these words in *Atlas Shrugged*, I was convinced I had discovered the key to my parents' failed marriage. It wasn't the incompatibility between my father and mother, although that didn't help. John was attracted to Mom because she embodied everything he valued in himself. The assessment was mutual.

Of course there was physical attraction. Two people don't have sex based on academic conclusions alone. But there it was, on the pages of *Atlas Shrugged*, the statement that foreshadowed the break-up of my family. The scene is one in which two of Rand's heroes, Francisco d'Anconia and Hank Rearden, speak about sex, love, and philosophy. Francisco says that sex is not a means to achieving self-esteem; it's a reflection of what he already has. Love is not blind, he says, or impervious to Reason. Sex is "the most profoundly selfish of all acts" because it cannot be performed except for one's own enjoyment, "in the confidence of being desired and being worthy of desire."[5] As Francisco describes it, what a man finds sexually attractive reveals his entire philosophy of life. The woman he sleeps with tells you his valuation of himself. Ayn Rand writes Francisco's words:

> The man who is proudly certain of his own value, will want the highest type of woman he can find, the woman he admires, the

strongest, the hardest to conquer—because only the possession of a heroine will give him the sense of an achievement, not the possession of a brainless slut ... He does not seek to gain his value, he seeks to express it. There is no conflict between the standards of his mind and the desires of his body.[6]

Now, at various places in her fiction, Rand inserts large portions of didactic monologue in the form of a speech or an expanded conversation. Some consider her style to be literarily irresponsible, but it gets the job done. In his "Sex Speech," Francisco describes two types. The first individual respects and exalts himself. He expresses confidence in himself, and is proudly certain of his own value. His sexual choice is the result and the sum of his fundamental convictions about himself. He wants the highest type of woman he can find, the woman he admires, the strongest, the hardest to conquer—because only the possession of a heroine will give him the sense of an achievement. The second person, Rand describes as a weak, spineless mass of contradictions who loathes himself. He's convinced of his own worthlessness, so he's drawn to a woman he despises—because she will "release him from that objective reality in which he is a fraud, she will give him a momentary illusion of his own value and a momentary escape from the moral code that damns him."[7]

My own view of sex has been whipsawed back and forth from the Objectivist view to the Victorian view. That trial has lasted my entire life. Victorians understood that sex was dangerous, kind of dirty, and something to hide. Like the Victorians, I believed the body was bad, or at least not as good as the intellect. In contrast, Ayn Rand's view of sex seemed unrestrictive, although her restrictions were actually substantial compared to the free love movement of the 60s and 70s, when the mantra was, "If it feels good, do it." She recognized a morality based on Reason that flowed from her view of herself to her choice of partner. The precondition of Reason and self-esteem allowed for a sound choice of sexual partner. There was commitment, just not marital commitment in the fundamentalist way that her theistic critics preach. Instead, the Objectivist shares a mutual commitment to his sexual partner: to a moral philosophy and the value of the Individual. Someone who views sex as merely a bodily experience does not, according to Rand, value sex highly enough.

Like Objectivists, I wanted freedom. College provided a venue for liberation, but it wasn't what I thought. My pursuit only highlighted my deeper confusion and pain. Intellectually, I have a liberated mindset, I couldn't forget. The old statements came back to haunt me. Because my sex life was a mess, it was hard to hear what Dad said about the "glory" of sex.

"Sex is not just a physical act, Dad said. "There is a lot more to it than that. It's an intimate connection between two people that goes beyond sensual. In the Bible, sex is a model and a foretaste of the relationship we will have with God." Dad said that Christians call it "oneness."

> There's more to sex than mere skin on skin. Sex is as much spiritual mystery as physical fact. As written in Scripture, "The two become one." Since we want to become spiritually one with the Master, we must not pursue the kind of sex that avoids commitment and intimacy, leaving us more lonely than ever—the kind of sex that can never "become one." There is a sense in which sexual sins are different from all others. In sexual sin we violate the sacredness of our own bodies, these bodies that were made for God-given and God-modeled love, for "becoming one" with another.
> — I Corinthians 6:16-7:5 (MSG)

From the biblical perspective, "oneness" is the word that sums up the purpose of sex. "I'll concede that the Gospel view of sex has restrictions," Dad continued. "One of the purposes is to glorify God, not self. But the pleasure that God intended and the intimacy He wants a couple to have is undeniable."

Meanwhile, I understood sex to be the most profoundly selfish of all acts: in Rand's words "an act which [one] cannot perform for any motive but [one's] own enjoyment."[8] In sex, she celebrated pride and admiration.

> *The highest expression of the most intense union of these two responses—pride and admiration—is romantic love. Its celebration is sex.*[9]

— Nathaniel Branden

Any Rand would say that we really are poor lovers if we do not love ourselves. There is a sense in which we love in others what we love in our selves. Few people are willing to talk about loving themselves. She wrote that our culture has trended toward self-abasing, to the point that she advocates "loving ourselves" explicitly.

John believed that. He would say, "The Golden Rule was at least half right, because Jesus assumed self-love as a starting point when he said, 'Love thy neighbor as thyself.' Treat others the way you want to be treated. It assumes you will treat others well, because you treat yourself well, and you want to be treated well."

No disagreement from Dad! "Paul the Apostle takes that thought even further," Dad said, "when he illustrates the marital relationship, 'No man ever treats his own body poorly. So don't treat your wife's body poorly; it is in fact your own.'"

Both Christianity and Objectivism see the beauty and intimacy in sex. Beginning in Genesis, the Bible says that the sexual "oneness" goes beyond the physical. Sexual unity is not less than the physical component, rather it's much more. "God paints us a picture of Himself through the unity and diversity of Man and Woman," Dad said. "Still, I can see why sex perpetuated your feeling of loneliness."

"What?" I sat up. His statement made no sense to me. "Doesn't the Bible say that sex is the answer to loneliness?" I was adamant. "What about when God created Adam and said, 'It's not good for man to be alone.' I thought that's when he created Eve."

He was calm, and he seemed to genuinely understand. "Look, it's absolutely natural for you to try to deal with loneliness through sex. It was originally designed, in part, as an antidote to loneliness. But there is a key. The only real cure for loneliness is what sex actually points to: intimacy with God through Jesus. Sex is an appetizer. What will fulfill you truly—the intimacy you really want—no human relationship can provide." He then went on to say something that I had never thought of before. "Sex in marriage is great, because someone knows you completely and loves you anyway. Sex is a way to give yourself to someone else and say 'I belong completely, exclusively, and entirely to you.' That's one reason God says 'Thou shalt not commit adultery.' You're completely naked and exposed—totally vulnerable—and not rejected. You're experiencing, on a human level, just a hint of what it's like to know the complete acceptance of Jesus. And not only that, God gives himself to you! It's not a one-way relationship; that's why Christians can say '*my* God.'"

Disordered Affections

Despite the pictures of divine intimacy, I couldn't help but focus on my own messy life. I admitted to Dad, "Every time I pursue sex to experience intimacy, it works backwards. Instead of making me less lonely, it makes me lonelier." I didn't really understand this at that point, but in desperation, sex was the idol I worshipped with the hope of receiving the love and acceptance I craved. Sex contented me in the moment, but that feeling of satisfaction had a short half-life.

Following Rand's advice in my moment of uncertainty, I "checked my premises." I was following my passions, but was I looking in the right place? Ayn Rand was spot on when she said, about all of us, that our desires are too weak. Dad was certainly in agreement with this. Many of us are not passionate and ambitious enough! We should nurture and pursue greater passion. Even Ayn Rand, however, didn't go far enough. "By extolling human achievement and the mind of the individual as the greatest virtue and production as the individual's most satisfying goal," Dad proposed, "Rand exchanges the ultimate for the penultimate. God, through Jesus Christ, is the final satisfaction of our deepest longing. A relationship with Him is the totality we're designed for." I was having a tough time with *human* relationships, so his "relationship" talk about God may have been lost on me.

I grew up with a destructive view of sex. It could have been my early exposure to pornography. It might have had something to do with my parents' divorce when I was eleven. Certainly, with my keen interest in Rand's writing, her own, somewhat explicit, depictions of sex could have formed my early understanding. But they didn't. Whatever it was, something got mixed up, and I ended up objectifying women and, as I have described, seeking sexuality as a way to overcome loneliness.

I didn't look for a sexual partner to reflect my own self-esteem and the positive qualities I saw in myself. I was much more like James Taggart in that respect: making himself feel better about himself, reaching out to Cherryl, a young waitress, trying to make her way in New York City. He wanted respect and admiration. He wanted to show his contempt for social stigma while at the same time using society's reaction to bolster his view of his own superiority. My motives were less complex, but no less misguided.

From both the Objectivist and the Christian viewpoint, I was looking to sex to do something it was not meant to. From the Objectivist perspective, I was reversing the law of cause and effect, trying to replace the mind by seizing the products of the mind, trying to gain self-esteem from sexual adventures. One of Rand's heroic producers in *Atlas Shrugged*, Francisco, says that the playboy is a man who despises himself. He tries to gain self-esteem from sexual adventures. Until college, my exploits were more fantasy than real. I didn't see a connection between my mind and my body. I viewed the sexual urges as disconnected from my intellect and my view of the world. If Ayn Rand could have spoken to me then, she probably would have told me to read Francisco's interchange with Hank Rearden in *Atlas Shrugged*. Francisco is a man of the mind, disguised as a playboy. Confiding in Hank Rearden, he explains that he has been promoting the persona of a playboy, but that's not really who he is. Someone with his Reason-based morality sees Reality for what it is. He knows that sex cannot be the answer to self-esteem, or success, or loneliness, any more than wealth stems from material resources and has no intellectual root or meaning. Sex is not a cause; it's an effect. The cause is a person's own self-image.

> *...a man's sexual choice is the result and the sum of his fundamental convictions. Tell me what a man finds sexually attractive and I will tell you his entire philosophy of life. Show me the woman he sleeps with and I will tell you his valuation of himself.*[10]

While there may have been a man who realized his perfect complement and the mirror of his own value in the pursuit of his lover, I was far from seeing my own value. Just as my understanding of Objectivist ideas has developed slowly over many years, my initial impressions of Christianity have evolved into something very different. It wasn't until years later that I came to articulate the contrast to the Objectivist view of sex.

In college, I studied Victorian Literature, especially poetry. What attracted me to that specific genre had a lot to do with what the Victorians were trying to accomplish. As my professor said, "These writers never tired of expressing the Gospel in a new and different way." Quite frankly, my classmates and I experienced that "new and different way" as opaque metaphors and obscure Biblical allusions. It was frustrating at best and, at its worst, futile. By that time, I had already been investigating Christianity, and I knew a lot. For a secular and liberal institution like Brown, I was an anomaly. I equated the Victorian mindset with Christianity across the board. My ability to track with these Victorians gave me an edge, and I picked my major.

I was looking for some way of explaining my parents' divorce, to simplify it. If I could translate the divorce into black and white and simplify or justify my rage and insecurity, maybe I could feel better. But it wasn't that simple. In John's case, I couldn't separate his actions from the man himself. I knew this man. I had embraced his world view, and looked into his soul. I had seen his genuine longing for goodness. I couldn't deny that the two aspects of my own world view were incompatible. Instead of clarifying, it confused me.

Philosophy of Sex

The Victorians recognized a duality between the mind and the body that was very Greek, but, as Dad was quick to point out, not Biblical. He was adamant in debunking the tendency towards the anti-corporeal. "The Bible affirms the material as *good*, from Creation. The Christian's destiny is material. Jesus talked about a material heaven." It turns out that Rand had a lot more in common with a biblical view of sex than the Victorians did.

The Platonic view of sex goes in the other direction: sex as animal passion. While it was much more influential in, say, the Victorian era, I came to think that the Christian view is just this: the body is bad and the spirit is good—the lower, physical, "animal" nature is chaotic and dark, and the higher, rational, "spiritual" nature is civilized and noble. This view led me to see sex as a degrading, dirty thing, a necessary evil for the propagation of the human race. In many traditional cultures, the idea of sex-as-dirty was attached to the primacy of the family as the highest good and the main way to obtain one's identity. Pre-marital sex was forbidden because it was dirty, and sex was only allowable for the "higher good" of having children and building up the family name. As I reached college age, my limited experience of the Christian church did nothing to dispel my view of sex as "dirty." The idea that "truly spiritual people should refrain from sex, or that sex was only right to do if you were trying to have children, or that sexual pleasure was not appropriate for high-minded people—or women—grew out of this basic view.

As I investigated the various, historical views on sexuality, I recognized their influence all around me. While the Greeks located the source of evil in the physical, the Romantics located it in culture. They thought human beings in their pristine, unspoiled, original state were brimming with natural goodness and creativity—it's only society that stifles it. Goodness is achieved by liberating the basic, primal instincts, which are in themselves pure. Victorianism opposed Romanticism by suppressing the primal instincts, which in themselves are evil.

While the first view sees sex as an inevitable biological drive and the second a necessary evil, the last view sees sex as a critical way of self-expression, a way to "be yourself" and "find yourself." For biological realists, all sex is "right" if it's safe. For Platonists, all sex is "wrong," tainted in some way. For Romantics, the quality of interpersonal love is the primary touchstone that makes sex right or wrong.

> *God saw all that he had made, and it was very good. And there was evening, and there was morning—the sixth day.*
> —*Genesis 1:31 (NIV)*

The Christian attitude toward sex is popularly thought to be the "Platonist" view, but it most definitely is not. It differs radically from each of these three competitors. Contrary to the Platonist view, the Bible teaches that sex is very, very good.

At any rate, I learned that from Dad. On the other hand, he learned Objectivism from me, perhaps more than he wanted. He listened because he cared about me. At least he knew enough to describe Christianity in terms of Objectivism. "Christianity is not some religious version of Objectivism," he said, "where the gods of the moralistic religions favor the success of the overachievers. It's not where the climbers of the moral ladder go to heaven. The God of the Bible is the one who comes down into this world to accomplish salvation and give us grace that we could never attain ourselves. He loves the unwanted. He loves the weak and the unloved. He's not just a king and we're not just his subjects. He's not merely a shepherd and we his sheep. He is a husband and we are his spouse. He is ravished with us; even those of us no one else notices."

Conclusion

Sex is powerful. Yet, we throw it around in our culture like it's simply a venue for pleasure or, alternatively, a degrading taboo that should be taken sparingly, if at all. Sex was neither for me, but it was more than I thought. And ultimately, I had to *think* about it. I had to understand where this most primal and intimate function of life fit. I was no more comfortable with casual sex than I was with a casual comprehension of sex. After numerous discussions with John, and as many with Dad, the fact was that my confusion about sex remained. Nevertheless, one undeniable fact was clear. My view of sex would be an extension of my philosophy, whatever that turned out to be.

4

MONEY

Money is the root of all evil.[1]

— Bertram Scudder

If you ask me to name the proudest distinction of Americans, I would choose—because it contains all the others—the fact that they were the people who created the phrase 'to make money.' ... Americans were the first to understand that wealth has to be created. The words 'to make money' hold the essence of human morality.[2]

— Francisco d'Anconia

If another topic challenges sex for a place in the annals of taboos, it's money. At most kitchen tables, family finances are generally the purview of parents only, and when kids are brought into the discussion, it is not uncommon that some amount of berating or guilt is involved. At dinner parties, we would never discuss how much we make or owe, but we sure want our friends to acknowledge the clothes, the phone, or the car we just bought. Some of us revel in the status of cost and others in the status of savings.

Like sex, we tend to obsess about money personally and even culturally, but it's rare to find someone with a well-honed, let alone well balanced, philosophy about money. More than that, I would argue, our obsession with it is tinged with a kind of schizophrenia. Our country is in a difficult recession, it's all we hear about on the news, yet the malls are packed every weekend. Statistically Americans give more to charity than any other country, and wealthy Americans the most, yet that same demographic is scourged for its alleged greed. We never think we have enough, but we don't like to save and we complain about others having too much.

Our relationship to money is alternately a relationship of the anorexic or the glutton. Either way, it's fundamentally obsessive, while simultaneously cloaked in denial.

Over the years, talks with my fathers congealed and converged into one long discourse about their differing views of the world. Rarely did they speak with each other directly, but a dialogue emerged between them, with me as the agent. They each spoke a language that was foreign to the other, and I was the interpreter. Not long into the Conversation, I concluded that pitting Rand against Christianity on the topic of money is a false contrast. Despite Rand's choice of language and Biblical references in her fiction and nonfiction, I don't think she intended it. The real contrast in *Atlas Shrugged* is between the producers and the looters. James Taggart, Dagny's older brother, expresses the anti-philosophy of Rand through his view of money.

Over and over, James and other detractors criticize Rand's heroes for their view of money. Rand purposely portrays the detractors cartoonishly, and in doing so, highlights the way her heroes are misunderstood. Nevertheless, James Taggart's sentiments resonate with people today. When the subject of money comes up, the antagonists react to what they perceive as greed, indiscretion, narrow-mindedness, lack of concern for others (emotional or otherwise), and stinginess.

Most people understand greed as an excessive desire to possess more than what one needs or deserves, especially with respect to material wealth. Greed is reprehensible acquisitiveness or an insatiable desire for wealth and, in the language of the religious, one of the seven deadly sins.

> *It seems to me that there are more important things in life than making money... [Money] is not the standard, it seems to me, by which one gauges a man's value to society.[3]*
>
> — James Taggart

While James Taggart's motives are unclear, he complains about greed because it disregards any benefit to society. That is James Taggart's standard of goodness. Of course, as the anti-hero, he lacks consistency. Later, he decides to manipulate government policy to make obscene amounts of money. He attempts to control the copper, transportation, and oil industries. As he plots, he is blind to the same qualities in himself that he vilifies in others.

In the interactions related to money, Rand's heroes are suspected of the worst possible motives. Rand makes no apology for any of these character traits in her heroes. She does not compel us to exalt them *in spite* of these, but *because* of them. If Dagny's detractors were right to vilify her and her world view, we might be able to stop here. But Rand shows us that her heroes' view of money—and their resulting actions—represent the essence of their virtue. Through Francisco d'Anconia—a copper industrialist and heir to an enormous fortune—Rand expresses the enthusiasm that characterizes her passion for Reason. Francisco is bigger than life; in fact, he is a lot like John.

...the root of all evil?

When John talks about "the love of money," he earnestly venerates the qualities that create wealth: a keen mind, technical skill, perseverance. The gleam in his eye belies his rich experience of productivity. Like Francisco, he belittles his detractors—with a measured, deliberate violence of thought— as they casually disdain his deeply held virtues.

John venerates Francisco's speech in *Atlas Shrugged* on the meaning of money." Money isn't just currency," he said. "The power and prestige that comes with money isn't even an end in itself. It goes deeper than that."

In complete agreement with the Christian perspective, Rand's heroes do not love money for its "comforts." Dagny works violently, sweating, in rugged conditions under heavy strain. She eschews the financial security that money can bring when she raises money, independently, for the John Galt Line. I asked John, "If not for money's comfort, then why work so hard?"

"I work so hard because of what money represents," he said. "Production is the essence of virtue. Making money means creating value and sustaining life."

Francisco's—and John's—perspective on money resonated. I derided the Christian viewpoint and its source, the Bible. I pressed Dad on the issue since the phrase, "love of money," originated with the New Testament. With the confidence of a Randian hero, I asked, "How can you say that money, or the love of it, is the root of all evil?" I explained Francisco's speech, and Dad showed me the passage from which it originated.

> *But godliness with contentment is great gain. For we brought nothing into the world, and we can take nothing out of it. But if we have food and clothing, we will be content with that. People who want to get rich fall into temptation and a trap and into many foolish and harmful desires that plunge men into ruin and destruction. For the love of money is a root of all kinds of evil.*

Some people, eager for money, have wandered from the faith and
pierced themselves with many griefs.
— I Timothy 6:6-10, 17-19 (MSG)

An amateur biblical scholar, Dad's passion for the Bible parallels John's passion for Rand's ideas. "The Bible is a sacred book," he said, "the Word of God."

In my mind, I thought biblical teaching was designed to eradicate anything that would contribute to my joy and self-fulfillment, especially in the realm of money. Before I read it, I figured that it said "money, or the love of it, is the root of all evil," but the message is much more nuanced than I expected.

When I shared Francisco's money speech with Dad, he said, "Francisco seems to understand the perspective of his detractors, but don't equate them with the Christian perspective. The Bible warns about what happens when human desires become out of balance, as in 'An inordinate desire for money is the root of all kinds of evil.' Money is not evil. Francisco's pecuniary values match up a lot more with the Bible than you think." Dad made it clear: "The Bible talks about wealth as a good thing. Wealthy individuals are all over the historical narrative. Abraham, Job, and Joseph are all rich through God's blessing. But, their lives illustrate that anything displacing God in the human heart and mind destroys the soul. God is Ultimate. If I esteem anything more highly than God, I will lose my spiritual footing completely and my life will be out of balance.[4] Money is a proxy for value. Money is good. Working for money is good. When it becomes "ultimate," it can destroy. It's not an ultimate thing, and it was never meant to be."

It might have sounded moralizing to an outsider, but it came from deep down, spiritual as it was. I reflected on Dad's perspective with a much less exalted analogy. Growing up, John took me to see the Philadelphia Eagles play. I loved the strategy and intensity of NFL football, as massive players collided on the field. The enthusiasm of the crowd drew me in, and the action on the field was intense. Occasionally, I glanced at the scoreboard—to check the time left or confirm the stats. Mostly, I was caught up in the progress of the team down the field toward the end zone. Money is like the scoreboard; it is not the most engaging part of the game. Everyone looked at the score. It was important. But I didn't come to see the scoreboard. Like that scoreboard, money is the tracking system, not the main event. The main event is the life that money facilitates.

In a flashback to their youth, Francisco shares wisdom to help Dagny define her work ethic and explain the source of her worth.

> *Dagny, there's nothing of any importance in life—except how well you do your work. Nothing. Only that. Whatever else you are, will come from that. It's the only measure of human value... When you grow up, you'll know what I mean.[5]*

Dagny's highest value is her capacity to work, and she measures it by what she produces. Her production comes from who she is, a thinking individual, with one sufficient and indispensable resource: her mind. Money is the measure, and from that, everything else flows.

What Money Buys

What we work for depends on what we value. Specifically, what gives us worth? What do we value above all else? If we value financial security, we hoard our money. If we value others' approval, we give away our money or buy gifts for others, effectively buying their approval. If being powerful defines our worth, we use the weight of our money to manipulate and control other people. How we use our money speaks volumes.

John's use of money impresses me; it speaks to his philosophy. He refuses to flaunt his money, but he uses it to achieve ends that are important to him. His wealth is the "James Bond" version. Not that he spends a lot on gadgets, but he has a taste for the finer things. Over the years, he has accumulated a portfolio of luxuries. At various times, he has purchased an authentic Vegas craps table, Rolex watches, a horse farm in Florida, complete with winning race horses, a private jet, and a second home. He drove a BMW because a Mercedes was "out of his station." Later he drove a Mercedes. He buys what *he* wants. He even buys himself a Christmas present in July, has it wrapped at the time of purchase, and puts it under the tree in early December. He has forgotten what he bought himself, so he's always surprised. But he knows that he will get at least one present he will like, from someone who knows him.

John chooses how to use money in a way that furthers his ability to be a producer. Perhaps the most important element of that statement is the "HE chooses…" While not everyone would agree with his choices, the point is that he decides.

I have often wondered what the Bergdorf Goodman salesman in the men's department thought when he saw John approaching—a well-dressed man meandering in. He could be browsing, but there is a twinkle in his eye that indicates a particular certainty. He knows his purpose. It won't take him long to get to the point. "I'd like to see your tailored section."

Understated, yet direct, John is thoughtful and circumspect. He calculates. He takes time and chooses carefully. The salesman at Bergdorf helps him pick out woolen weaves that feel like silk and look like deep velvet.

When the suits are tailored, they fit him perfectly: standard suits, with a slight Italian flair, not inconsistent with a man of his age. Sometimes an English cut, with three buttons down the front that make him look taller. Never double-breasted. When the salesman disappears, we wander into another section of the men's store, I naively suggest, "What about that suit? I've never seen you wear anything like that," pointing to a mannequin wearing a dark, double-breasted suit with pinstripes. Effortlessly, John launches into an Italian, South Philly accent. "Eh!" He flicks his four fingers under his chin. Speaking out of one side of his mouth, "Whad'a you kiddin' me?" Eyebrows up, "An Italiano wit' pin-stripes!? Any respectable joint would peg me at the door!" We both laugh.

Shirts are another story. These are John's signature. Unlike the shirts of mere mortals, his have no buttons. At least, none you can see. Just a smooth finish from neck to waist, down the center of his person; the button

> *John knows that peoples' impressions matter. He presents an image to reinforce his ability to produce.*

holes hide underneath the tab. With carefully chosen ties to match, he looks stellar. All said, John purchases ten suits, each with multiple pairs of trousers, several sport coats, multiple pair of casual pants, ties, belts, cuff links, socks, and sweaters. He repeats this process every ten years.

The next week, we stop in to pick up some of the remaining sportswear that John had purchased. By this time, John has made friends with the tailor, the department manager, and the entire Men's Store staff. As the salesman carefully places the tailored pants and jackets into the lined covers that protect the clothing, he confirms that all of the combinations are coded by color and pattern, like a wealthy adult version of "Garanimals."

"Why the fuss?" I asked him once. "Why spend so much time and effort and money on appearance?"

It's not because "clothes make the man." It's because John wants to make a statement. He wants to reflect who he is to himself, and to others, because he is a producer, one who uses his mind to create value. "The man makes the man," he says," but the clothes follow." A man's appearance is what people see. It would be stupid to ignore that, or at the very least, counterproductive to one's goals. Image is a tool. It sets an expectation, if you know what you're doing." John knows that peoples' impressions matter. He presents an image to reinforce his ability to produce. "You avoid a lot of unnecessary persuasion and gain credibility," he said, "by making a good impression from the start." Money, for John, is the means to an end.

What Dad values is both similar and different from John. The status of having money or not having money does not carry much weight with Dad. There have been periods in his life when he made lots of money, but lost it. Lots of hard work later, he still had none. Through his experiences—as much as through Christian doctrine—Dad has "learned to be content in whatever his circumstances."[6] His life is simple. He has what he needs: not a lot. Living alone on a farm that he has paid for through sweat and tears, Dad grows his own food, milks his own cows, and trades for what he lacks. His annual income rounds to zero. What little money he has, he spends on the farm itself. Over the years, he has developed a vision for the farm as a training ground for missionaries. He dreams of helping people who want to help others improve their quality of life. He envisions translating the technology and resources he cultivates on the farm to other rural environments: solar energy, greenhouses, wells, crops, ponds, and animals. I used to think it was because he was naive or, worse, compelled to earn favor with God by doing good. Inside I thought, "What a waste of a life. Ayn Rand would have considered this a failure of epic proportions, characterized by everything he's missing." Admittedly, I may have missed something.

"I have experienced the greatest possible joy in my life with Jesus," he said. "And I want to be where He is. I see Him working in the lives of people, and I want to join Him in the work He is doing." His decisions about money reflect his highest passion: experiencing God and his glory. In his words, "Why settle for less?"

It would be easy to observe my fathers from the outside and deduce they were each compelled by money issues. One the glutton; the other, the anorexic. In my own misunderstanding of Dad's choices, I certainly had characterized him as the latter. While John was not a glutton, his moderation was not obvious to me. Yet, over time and through our discussions, I realized they were both led distinctly by principle. In coming to understand those principles—Biblical and Objectivist—I realized that the matter of principle was the point. In this as other areas, it was the fact of guiding principles, or world view that was significant, because as I looked around at plenty of other people, they had no guiding principles about money.

Taking It

John has the two conversational voices. Sometimes he uses lots of "Yo!"talking "wit' da hands," and "Hey you…Yeah you!" He sounds like a city kid from the Italian section of Philadelphia, which he happens to be. Other times, he speaks with perfect waspy diction. Gray hair in all the right places, finely tailored suits, and just the right amount of posture: not too erect as to appear uptight, but not slumping either. He's relaxed, or indifferent, never hyper. He carries himself like the quintessential town mayor, which he happens to be. Every one of John's *experiences* help form his philosophy, but they also comprise testing grounds. He lives as a producer, and he continually tests his ability to produce. From the first whisper of an idea to its integration into his philosophy, he tests its real world practicality, like a test-marketer assessing product demand. Does this feature appeal to the market? Does that aspect work? I learned that highly effective producers do what they do for the purpose of producing. Sometimes that means connecting with people. Sometimes that means doing the Italian thing, and sometimes it means something else. Producers make the most of the situation. If it benefits him to be a certain way in a certain crowd, he will be… within reason.

John does not believe in lying, cheating, or stealing to make a buck. He talks a lot about character. We may disagree about ethical particulars, but John has boundaries. He cringes when the media characterizes the "greedy businessman" as normative, as if they are all devoid of morality and focused on hoarding wealth as a game. "Gordon Gekko was a loser," John said, "but he was misunderstood, too."

Gordon Gekko, the anti-hero in the movie *Wall Street*, is notorious for his adage, "Greed is good." He made some viewers recoil and others cheer. Gordon Gekko professes a passion for money and for the enhancement of his life as an individual. He purports to align with the incentives of the other shareholders instead of the motives of the board, which are pitifully "altruistic," if not deceitful and negligent.

> *The point is, ladies and gentlemen, that greed—for lack of a better word—is good. Greed is right. Greed works. Greed clarifies, cuts through, and captures the essence of the evolutionary spirit. Greed, in all of its forms—greed for life, for money, for love, knowledge—has marked the upward surge of mankind. And greed—you mark my words—will not only save Teldar Paper, but that other malfunctioning corporation called the U. S. A. Thank you very much.*[7]
>
> — Gordon Gekko

Greed typically denotes an excessive, extreme desire for something, usually money. It's often uncomplimentary. While the love of money is typically equated with greed, that is not the definition Francisco intended to exalt. His idea was not, as in the New Testament, an over-desire that is condemned as a distraction, a distortion, or a venial sin. To the extent that Gekko's intentions align with Reason, hard work, and diligence instead of trickery and deceit, he sides with Francisco and his love of money.

Ironically, Francisco may well have resonated with another character from *Wall Street*, Carl Fox, played by Martin Sheen. Towards the end of the movie he says, "Stop going for the easy buck and start producing something with your life. Create, instead of living off the buying and selling of others."[8] This character plays the hard-working, wise, salt-of-the-earth father figure against Gordon Gekko's arrogant, money-hungry trader. But, the wisdom of Carl Fox that prevails in the end reveals a hard-working, persevering craftsman. Gekko is neither a producer nor a creator of value;

he merely moves money from one stack to the other. Carl Fox and his colleagues at BlueStar Airline create value.

Property, wealth, or value sustains or enhances one's life. "Life, liberty, and the pursuit of happiness" is indeed a fundamental, inalienable right, as Rand sees it. Taking another's property by force or fraud is tantamount to taking their life, the ultimate violation of their fundamental rights. John has said, many times, "Principles make the man." He also said "Actions make the man," so I think he means that the two should be consistent. By his reasoning, it is the nature of Man to live by Reason and not by force. To live by force means to live as an animal, whose instinct dictates its actions. To live as a man is to live by Reason. Living otherwise—as a barbarian or worse—does not allow a person to live a life of integrity. Integrity is important to John; maybe even more important than how others view him and his money.

Making It

Unlike the taboo in many families, "making money" was a frequent topic at our kitchen table (or any table for that matter). As a family, we frequent Uncle Bill's Pancake House every summer at the Jersey shore. Each year, a new crop of freshly-scrubbed teenage girls take summer jobs waiting tables. The first Saturday morning of the season, we were characteristically engaged in a heated conversation about the value of work. When the fifteen-year-old girl in the Uncle Bill's uniform came to take our order, John didn't miss a beat. With a feigned look of seriousness, he says, "I want you to know that I *earn* every penny I make." He smiles. The girl is nonplussed. What he means to say is this: he works hard and uses his mind. His money is not the fruit of someone else's labor. Were he to inherit or cheat his way to wealth, he would not make that statement. I thought at the time he was trying to be a Randian character and, in that moment, I felt a little self-conscious. Despite his quirky forwardness, John is a man of integrity.

Dad's quirkiness takes a different form. Most of the time, his sense of fashion is limited to torn overalls, gray t-shirts, and oil-stained work boots. I admit that I recoil when he goes into town. Strangers respond with disapproval and disdain. Yet, when I shake his calloused hand and gaze at the creases of work in his forehead, I remember what is most important, that he is a survivor. Even Ayn Rand venerates the self-sustaining minority of individuals who feed the country with their production. In *Atlas Shrugged*, she profiles one of the last bastions of Capitalism, the ultimate entrepreneurs: farmers.

His work ethic extended beyond his life on the farm. When my parents were young and my sister and I were still toddlers, we moved to Sheffield Road, a 1950s development where the houses sat close together, but not cramped. While completing his dissertation, he worked several jobs to support his family. He waited tables, taught swimming and advanced scuba, laid down subway track, and re-shingled roofs. Work, for Dad, has always been a way of life.

Anthony, slightly younger than Dad, was one of the first neighbors we met. Muscular and athletic, Anthony was not your typical college student. A rugby player, he had broken his nose three times and each knee twice. Anthony worked hard and played hard. With sharp reflexes and keen senses, he was intense, and almost instantly, Dad and Anthony knew they were the same. When the mercury rose to unprecedented heights in the summer of 1974, Anthony's roofing business suffered from an understandable, but unforeseen, shortage of laborers. Dad heeded the call, as much to spend time with Anthony as for the extra bucks. He worked hard, not just for his age, but for anyone at any age. Far from a "necessary evil," work for Dad was life-enhancing.

I myself have never experienced financial security. I cannot tell you what it feels like to have certainty about my financial future, to know that my family will be free from financial burdens, whether or not I lose my job.

But between Dad and John, I have watched financial fortunes made and lost, many times over. Dad—the most intense, intelligent, hard working man I have ever met—has made and lost more money than I will ever see. My experiences with him have been in the lean times. John is savvy, but not so transparent that you would know he is savvy. You can watch him forever, and still never "get" how John does what he does. My experiences with John have been mostly in times of plenty. Each man has known success and failure. Each has taught me through his response to looming financial failure.

Losing It

While he has risen to high positions at companies, I have never seen Dad with a lot of money. I *have* seen him without. When I came home from college one Christmas, Dad had just returned to the farm. An investment in California had gone very bad, and leaving balmy San Diego with his wife Debbie and their newborn son, he returned to the farm with nothing. During one of the leanest and coldest Christmases I can remember, we itemized the furniture as well as the nostalgia that had been stolen from the farm while he was away. The television, antique cabinets, tables, and chairs—even the wood-burning stove—were gone. The word "disappointment" doesn't come close to what I saw in Dad. Yet, for all the hurt and anger, there was never despair. While he had the sense that he would get through, neither one of us knew how that would happen.

"If my efforts don't 'click' by January," he said, "I will take the first job I find locally." In California, he was the president of a public company. He had been exploring similar positions. By January, nothing had clicked. A new General Motors plant, less than sixty miles from the farm, was looking for workers on the assembly line. He was over-qualified with a college degree, let alone a PhD, but he needed the job, and nobody asked.

His fortunes had gone from high to low. It was always like that for Dad, and yet, he was rock-steady. Not that he kept it inside; he told me exactly what he thought and how he felt. But he was the same man. I know how he viewed money, not just because he told me. I know because I saw it in his life. Money was important—I saw how he struggled—but not life-defining. The lack of money, or food, or heat was stressful, but he never lost his family or his passion. In all of his success, he never defined himself by success. And in the depths of failure, he rose above it.

I heard an illustration once that defined Dad's approach to the problems he encountered. Imagine yourself in a boat headed downstream, with cliffs on either side. As the river narrows, and you feel the cliffs closing in, you see an enormous rock rising out of the center of the river, such that you're unable to pass to the right or the left. Your boat will be destroyed by the boulder. At that moment, there are two ways you can pray. You can ask God to remove the rock, so that you won't be crushed, or you can pray, "God, please raise the water level so that I rise above it and pass safely." Dad has always chosen the latter course of action.

Not being a man of prayer, John dealt with adversity differently. One of his worst moments had to be when his airline was facing bankruptcy. Creditors at his door, threatening to take down the company, John fought bitterly to avoid the inevitable. Becoming his own hero, he did not throw himself on the mercy of the legal system that would have allowed him to default on his obligation. The banks had no leniency, no tolerance. At great expense to himself, he ploughed more money into the sinking business, paid his debt, and retained nothing but the honor of survival, and a clear conscience. But along the way, I saw the stress take its toll. I think we all did.

The lack of money, or food, or heat was stressful, but he never lost his family or his passion.

I cannot imagine John's burden. With the prospect of losing his financial security, he became bitter. His temper raged, and he lashed out. Family vacations at the Jersey shore became unbearable for his children. As the company's success eluded him, he grasped for anything he could still control: his vacation home, his family, his relationships. Even the grandchildren felt the stress and strain.

During that period, I came to understand the difference between "lovers of money" and "trusters of money." "Lovers" are those who find themselves daydreaming and fantasizing about new ways to make money, new possessions to buy, and looking with jealousy on those who have more than they do. For most of the time that I have known him, John has never really been that kind of a guy. On the other hand, "trusters" feel they have control of their lives and are safe and secure particularly because of their wealth. That has always been the case with John. There's a subtle line between working to make money and living for money. Earning money is a noble pursuit. The freedom to create value is at the heart of Capitalism. Just over that fine line, however, a slippery slope leads to slavery. We become enslaved to a deeper need: something which, when satisfied, justifies our existence and, when left unanswered, makes life unbearable.

"I look to Jesus and what he says about me," Dad explained. "The Gospel says that I am more poverty-stricken than I ever dared believe, but in Jesus Christ, I am more valuable than I ever dared hope. Money is important; just not the ultimate source of my peace and happiness."

In a flashback, Francisco says

> *"When I die, I hope to go to heaven—whatever the hell that is—and I want to be able to afford the price of admission."*
> *"Virtue is the price of admission," Jim said haughtily.*
> *"That's what I mean, James. So I want to be prepared to claim the greatest virtue of all—that I was a man who made money."*[9]

If productiveness is the ultimate measure of worth, then making money is the highest of virtues, and John's passions are rightly placed. But if God is the ultimate occupation of the human soul, then Dad's passion to get the most of God is the human's highest goal. Instead of using earned wealth to enhance his life with material comforts, the Bible offers a life-enhancement scheme that takes it to another level altogether.

> *The kingdom of heaven is like treasure hidden in a field. When a man found it, he hid it again, and then in his joy went and sold all he had and bought that field.*
>
> *Again, the kingdom of heaven is like a merchant looking for fine pearls. When he found one of great value, he went away and sold everything he had and bought it.*
>
> — Matthew 13:44-46 (NIV)

Jesus does not say blandly that treasure in heaven results from our generosity on earth. More passionately, he urges his followers to pursue treasure in heaven, the way a thirsty desert wanderer pursues water, or a savvy portfolio manager scours the financial landscape for investments. John comes nowhere close to the Biblical conclusion. Not through faulty reasoning, but the Objectivist simply starts from a different premise. That premise leads him to the "primacy of the individual."[10]

Dad says the premise and the logic are flawed.

Conclusion

The key takeaway for me is not that one view rejects money and the other embraces it. John and Dad agree on practically every function of money in society: a currency for trade, a measure of value, and a vehicle to store wealth. Yet they disagree on where money falls in the hierarchy of values. John sees it at the top, because it supports the life of the individual. Dad sees it further down—not because he values the individual less—because he values God above all else.

I admire Dad's choices; I appreciate the simplicity and his life's clarity, though John's view of money and its support of the individual have drawn me more toward Rand's conclusions. I understand the dangers of money and its potential to enslave, but Rand's detractors go too far. I reject their caricatures and their misunderstanding of money in her context. Yet more than anything, I am grateful that both my fathers are mindful of how they relate to money, and I am glad they discussed their ideas with me. Our discussions have provoked further reflection, and I have learned that I am responsible to be equally mindful. The contrasts between them may seem—may in fact *be*—stark, but those very contrasts have been a gift to me. I have no justification to live in denial about how I view money or how I use money. As in all things, intentionality, I discovered, is critical in the pursuit of Reason and Faith.

5

CAPITALISM

Of all the social systems in mankind's history, capitalism is the only system based on an objective theory of values.[1]

— Ayn Rand

With economic turmoil and volatility in the capital markets today, skeptics come out of the woodwork like bugs in an old farmhouse. They question the validity and the viability of Capitalism, particularly the idea of laissez-faire, that the state should not intrude in the economic activities of entities in a free market. Media commentators reference the invalidation of a "free-market economy." What G. K. Chesterton once said about Christianity can easily be addressed to today's critics of laissez-faire Capitalism in the

West: laissez-faire Capitalism has not been tried and found wanting. Rather, its moral basis has not been found "palatable" so it has not been tried.[2]

Capitalism is Rand's political system. She defines Capitalism in terms of the fundamental building blocks: a social system based on the recognition of individual rights, including property rights, in which all property is privately owned.[3]

John's Capitalism

"My world view doesn't allow for another economic or political structure. Laissez-faire Capitalism is its only alternative." It was John's professional, business tone. He put it on when he was saying something authoritative or academic, especially when we watched the talking heads on Sunday morning. In the realm of political economics, it was unnecessary; I have never questioned John's commitment to laissez-faire Capitalism.

Switching to his South Philly accent, he said with considerably more volume, "It means that you say to the government, 'Yo! Keep a' you' hands off my stuff!'" He turns to me, "You know what I'm sayin', boy!" His hands gesture to the imaginary governmental body behind the television image of the Capitol. I picture him yelling at Wesley Mouch and his cronies, villains from *Atlas Shrugged*. At best, they are misguided, but Ayn Rand makes no attempt to humanize them; they are unadulterated evil. They push an agenda whereby the government redistributes wealth, controls the means of production, and enacts laws that penalize the creation of value. Watching a liberal talking-head, John throws up his hands and shouts at the television, as if a referee just missed a foul against one of his beloved Sixers. To an outside observer—there are none—his words seem like a worker on a picket line, heckling a management spokesman. I know better. I think to myself, "I am an insider. I'm in the know." Because of the kitchen table monologues, I understand the philosophy underlying his frustration.

"A Collectivist government gets away with stealing!" he said. "And that, in the name of 'compassion!' Tell me where the compassion is in taking away an individual's hard-earned value." His tone demanded an answer to what was obviously rhetorical. "No one gets to trample on the rights of another individual. The government should be protecting my rights, not trampling on them." And then he said, "It ain't right."

When he wants to emphasize the simplicity and incontrovertible logic of his conclusion, he reverts to the street vernacular of his South Philly roots, even the accent. The more passionate, the more hand movement. It was John's unique way of expressing Ayn Rand's philosophy. What Ayn Rand did with prose, John accomplished with manual flourish. What he emphasized with passionate emotion, she communicated with tight, and sometimes biting, logic: not in sarcasm, but in compelling passages.

One of Rand's most powerful illustrations in *Atlas Shrugged* describes the Twentieth Century Motor Company. The story makes my blood boil every time I read it. The heroes become victims of what Rand calls the faulty philosophy of the Collectivist Ideal. Dagny Taggart, the heroine of *Atlas Shrugged*, discovers a motor that takes static electricity from the atmosphere and converts it into usable energy. She is beyond intrigued. She scours the country for the architect of this marvel. In a chance encounter on one of her rails, she meets a tramp, a casualty of failed businesses in the increasingly government-run economy. Through him, she learns the story of the factory's rise and fall. Its success and failure hinge on philosophy. Capitalist principles propelled the company to its apex; Collectivism presided over its downfall.

As the history of the company unfolds through multiple scenes, we get a distinct "Before-and-After" picture that mirrors the state of the country. At its height, the Twentieth Century Motor Company operated under Capitalism: individual merit, reward for performance, and positive competition. Under the direction of its founder, the company produced dependable, efficient motors that outperformed and outlasted the competition. When the owner died, his heirs attempted to run the company on socialist-altruistic principles, in which everybody works according to his ability and gets paid according to his need. As the once-proud, hard-working foreman, the tramp recounts the painful history of the factory. What started as a good intention in the mind of the heirs resulted in humiliation and disgrace for him, and for his peers.

> *Do you know how it worked, that plan, and what it did to people? ...the harder you work the more is demanded of you...—for anyone anywhere around you—it's theirs to receive, from diapers to dentures—and yours to work... for the whole of your life, without rest, without hope, without end..... From each according to his ability, to each according to his need.*[4]

Dad and John disagree about a lot, but not politics. After the divorce, I doubt they conversed with each other about the trivialities of politics, but they definitely talked to me. As far back as I can remember, their voting record lined up perfectly. When my vote diverged from Dad's, it diverged from John's and vice versa. The heat of politically charged debate among my family members was some of the hottest. The passion of these men set the Conversation ablaze, but the embers came from a different source in each man's world view.

John's philosophy *incorporates* Capitalism. For Dad, Capitalism was not part of his philosophy; it simply made sense. Dad quoted Scripture like he was referring to something he had read that morning, which he probably had. "When Paul the Apostle said, 'All things are lawful, but not everything is expedient,' I don't think he was thinking of Capitalism," Dad said when we were discussing politics and economics. "But you could apply that evaluation to political systems. Capitalism is expedient. It's not necessary for Christianity to thrive, but it addresses some fundamentals that Christianity uniquely understands."

As I conveyed Rand's thinking to Dad, he responded in agreement. "Rand's arguments for Capitalism make logical sense," he said. "But she doesn't explain the reason such arguments *must* be made in the first place. If thinking and rational self-interest is appropriate to human survival, then why do men behave in any other way? The Bible explains that our separation from God has curtailed our reason, among other things." He chuckled before he said, "In my experience, people are not always rational and consistent."

You know," Dad pondered, "I think Capitalism is the only system that makes room for this doctrine, and doesn't depend on the kindhearted benevolence of humanity."

Rand predicted the current political and economic environment—what she would characterize as an epidemic of irrationality. Thinking, or Reason, is an act of the will, unlike the autonomic reflex of an animal's survival instinct. Man has a different mode of survival. "So, why doesn't everyone fall in line with the thinking that is required for man's survival?" I asked John.

He answered without hesitation. "Bad philosophy. When people avoid what is in their rational self-interest, they reject Capitalism, because Capitalism rewards you when you act in your rational self-interest; Socialism rewards you if you don't. What's more, Socialism counts on people acting in each other's best interest. That's just not what makes people tick. Not for me, at least."

The logic of Christianity and Capitalism became clearer to me. If people will naturally be self-centered, and act according to what they believe will benefit themselves, then the best political and economic system is one which succeeds in that environment. The Socialist system requires that each individual act out of selfless, altruistic motives. It sounds nice, but the only way that could happen is if Man were innately centered on others. I agree with John. "It doesn't hold true in real life, any more than in *Atlas Shrugged.*" Every character is motivated by self-interest: John Galt, Dagny, Rearden, James Taggart... even the bum that rolls over with shiftless indignation when James tosses him a hundred dollar bill. There is a pivotal difference, however, between the self-interest of her heroes and that of her villains. The actions of one group are rational, founded in Reality. Since Rand sees that Capitalism aligns with Reality better than any other economic system, she concludes that the rationally self-interested thrive more in a Capitalist system than in any other. Those who neglect their rational self-interest will, according to Rand, settle for something less. That's not a threat; it's Reality. Actions have consequences.

> *The Socialist system requires that each individual act out of selfless, altruistic motives. It sounds nice, but the only way that could happen is if Man were innately centered on others.*

While my fathers' voting records aligned, their capitalistic, free market, limited government leanings budded from different soil. For John, Capitalism is the inevitable outflow of Rand's thought; rational self-interest, individual right to liberty, and the glory of production lead to the politics of Capitalism. For all the reasons that John espouses Capitalism, Dad agrees that Capitalism works. But Dad sees something in the rebellious nature of Man that dooms Collectivism.

Rand reacts violently to the Christian doctrine of Original Sin. In what she called the most definitive description of her philosophy—John Galt's 60-page speech in *Atlas Shrugged*—Rand's hero argues forcefully against the naysayers of human potential.

> *What is the nature of the guilt that your teachers call his Original Sin? What are the evils man acquired when he fell from a state they consider perfection? Their myth declares that he ate the fruit of the tree of knowledge—he acquired a mind and became a rational being. It was the knowledge of good and evil—he became a moral being. He was sentenced to earn his bread by his labor—he became a productive being. He was sentenced to*

experience desire—he acquired the capacity of sexual enjoyment. The evils for which they damn him are reason, morality, creativeness; joy—all the cardinal values of his existence. It is not his vices that their myth of man's fall is designed to explain and condemn, it is not his errors that they hold as his guilt, but the essence of his nature as man. Whatever he was—that robot in the Garden of Eden, who existed without mind, without values, without labor, without love—he was not man.[5]

Earlier in Galt's speech, Rand exalts rational morality, productiveness, passion, creativity, and joy. She denounces whatever condemns these virtues. She states emphatically that Man's "perfection" is not found in ignorance, sloth, complacency, and loveless sobriety. I shared this passage with Dad. He explained to me that while Rand's reference originates in Genesis, the Bible does not describe human beings as robotic in any way; rather, it is their very capacity to choose that is pivotal to the plot.

Whether Rand was denouncing Christianity or simply making a point about the demeaning cultural and philosophical tone of the world in *Atlas Shrugged*, Dad understands Genesis in a different way. His interpretation is, and has always been, life-affirming. He highlights the virtues of knowledge. "Knowing good and evil is not exclusively the domain of disobedience and rebellion." He recalls what an obedient kid I was, saying, "When you do something right, it becomes its own reward. We know—at least, it's possible to know—good and evil by doing good, as well as by doing evil. It happens all the time. Last week I took the alternator on the tractor to my friend, Donny, who is a mechanic. He fixed it for me, and told me to reinstall it myself. 'It's easy,' he said. 'Just connect the green wire to the left node and wrap the red wire around the remaining connection.' That went fine; Donny knows what he's doing. Now, if I had done the opposite, I would have destroyed the alternator. It was clearly my choice: my tractor, my alternator.

Whichever way I chose, I would have eventually found out the right way to do it. I didn't have to destroy the alternator to gain that knowledge."

Dad articulates all of this in his world view, and furthermore, he sees something that Ayn Rand misses. "Rand seems to understand, correctly, that the doctrine of Original Sin does not mean human beings are comprehensively and abjectly bad. What she does not understand, though, is that these 'cardinal values' of our existence were not designed to function independent of their Designer. They only work in the proper environment. Christians believe that humans naturally rebel against God, to our own detriment."

If kitchen appliances were animated, as Dad's analogy goes, we would be likened to that refrigerator, stubbornly refusing to be plugged into its power source. Disconnected, the refrigerator cannot work properly, according to its design. Similarly, we do not function optimally without our Power Source.

Work Ethic

Productiveness is the virtue of creating material values. In a free market, such a virtue is a necessity; there are no governmental bonuses for parasites. Contrary to another Big Lie, the rule of capitalist society, as of nature, is: he who does not work shall not eat. Capitalism is the system of productiveness; it is the system of and for producers... In a free society, only producers are consumers.[6]

Despite the source, Dad unequivocally agrees with this statement about the virtue of work. In fact, long before Leonard Peikoff wrote this passage in *Objectivism: The Philosophy of Ayn Rand*, Dad quoted the Apostle Paul's words from a letter to the church in first-century Greece: "He who does not work shall not eat."[7]

Objectivism and Christianity disagree on where money falls in the hierarchy of values. Objectivists see it at or close to the top because it supports the life of the individual. Christians see it down the hierarchy, not because Christians value the individual any less, but because they value God above all else. While the practical out-workings of each perspective may look similar, the core filter that precipitates each of the respective actions is different. Both value achievement and production. Both can be good Capitalists. But the Objectivist's choices will value and exalt the worth of the Individual, while the choices of a Christian will exalt the worth of God. The Objectivist idea of virtue is closely linked to work and production.

> *Both can be good Capitalists. But the Objectivist's choices will value and exalt the worth of the Individual, while the choices of a Christian will exalt the worth of God.*

As a Christian, Dad's work ethic traces back to what God has given Man to do. Work is good, not just to make money but to be human. "As human beings," he said, "we are designed to work. In Genesis, God gave Man the task of tending the garden, working the soil to produce what was needed for food. God provided that work for us, not because He couldn't have given us a handout, not because work was punishment, but because He designed us to work. Work has been good from the beginning."

Ayn Rand would concur that work is "good," but primarily as a means to an end: creating value. While she rejects the notion of a Creator, she articulates our industriousness in ways Dad would agree with.

Capitalism demands the best of every man—his rationality—and rewards him accordingly. It leaves every man free to choose the work he likes, to specialize in it, to trade his product for the products of others, and to go as far on the road of achievement as his ability and ambition will carry him. His success depends on the objective value of his work and on the rationality of those who recognize that value.[8]

And what is the result, according to Rand, of a Capitalist system?

When men are free to trade, with reason and reality as their only arbiter, when no man may use physical force to extort the consent of another, it is the best product and the best judgment that win in every field of human endeavor, and raise the standard of living—and of thought—ever higher for all those who take part in mankind's productive activity.[9]

Government

Ayn Rand is criticized for limiting the government's rightful role. True, her Capitalism requires "laissez-faire" to accurately reflect her understanding and intention; but she was *not* an anarchist.

I don't see it. It's a backward, primitive, unenlightened place. They don't even have a modern government. It's the worst government in any state. The laziest. It does nothing—outside of keeping law courts and a police department. It doesn't do anything for the people. It doesn't help anybody. I don't see why all our best companies want to run there.[10]

— Horace Bussby Mowen[11]

John values limited government pragmatically and on principle. As a practical matter, when free market participants invest intellectual or financial capital, they produce more wealth than the government with the same resources. On principle, the government's role is to protect the rights of individuals from criminals at home and abroad. It steps outside its role when it thinks about redistributing wealth (taking property by force) or controlling the means of production.

Dad agrees, but he also sees the government overstepping when the state tries to be the People's Benefactor. Step aside; laissez-faire. Dad is perfectly content to exercise his own will to benefit disenfranchised widows and orphans. In fact, he believes that all Christians should consider doing the same. I was surprised to hear his rationale. His "good works" (my description, not his) do not arise from an altruistic sense of duty to his fellow humans. Rather, he genuinely longs to join God in the work He is doing in the world. He has told me about experiencing God on numerous occasions, especially looking for where God is working, and joining Him. "I can't overstate my thrill at experiencing Jesus. That's my motivation, and not some sense of earning heaven, or earning anything. Heaven and my standing with God are secure because of what Jesus has already done. I want to be wherever He is, doing whatever He's doing."

Mom told me a story about when I was four years old and Dad was finishing his doctoral dissertation. As I descended the stairs to the basement where Dad was working, she saw me carrying a stack of paper and crayons. She asked what I was doing and I said, "I'm going to work on my dissertation." I am sure I didn't know what a dissertation was, but I knew it was something Dad was doing, and I wanted to be with him. I wanted to do what he was doing because I wanted to enter into his life.

With John, it was golf at the local "Chip and Putt." I never tired of it. For his part, he could have been out on the course playing eighteen holes with the guys, but he was throwing away a Saturday morning with me. I was thirteen years old, but when John held my club from behind, I putted like a pro.

Collectivism

In today's society, it seems morally distasteful to repel hard work. White collar men are often characterized as paper pushers, while blue collar workers are seen as "salt of the earth" types. While Rand's heroes in *Atlas Shrugged* are businessmen, so are her villains. James Taggart (titular head of Taggart Transcontinental Railroad), Eugene Lawson (former head of Community

National Bank), and Orren Boyle (President of Associated Steel) are businessmen who attempt to engineer the country's path out of crisis. They meet with Wesley Mouch, Floyd Ferris, and Mr. Thompson, the Head of State, in a continuing quest to expand the control of the State over industry and production. Their discussion addresses what Rand considers the anti-work ethic.

> *"It's [the productive individual's] lack of social spirit. They refuse to recognize that production is not a private choice, but a public duty... They've got to go on producing. It's a social imperative. A man's work is not a personal matter, it's a social matter."[12]*
> *"The only justification of private property," said Orren Boyle, "is public service."[13]*

If I ever want to get John riled up and launch him into a tirade, I know what buttons to push. I need only *hint* that it *might* be appropriate for corporations to "give something back" because of what they have *received* from society. He will go on for days. Businessmen generate wealth, create jobs, and make life better for everyone through their innovation and enterprise. The idea that these human beings are somehow indebted to the Collective is anathema.

Instead of inhibiting rationality and denouncing achievement, John Galt urges his hearers to exalt the mind and its productive capacity. Capitalism, not Collectivism, makes Rand's ideal world possible, wherein everyone pronounces the oath "I swear—by my life and my love of it—that I will never live for the sake of another man, nor ask another man to live for mine."

Assessing Dad and John is certainly much more nuanced than the distinctions between a Collectivist and a Capitalist. While they agree on Capitalism, neither sees Capitalism as an end in itself. John sees it as the man-made outflow of rationally self-interested individuals. Laissez-faire Capitalism is a means to honor the Objectivist's Ideal Man. Dad's desire to glorify and enjoy God happens outside of politics. "No man-made economic or political system approaches God's glory," he said, "but Capitalism works for the simple fact that individuals are inherently selfish. Originally created in God's image, we have all gone our own way, like the refrigerator that insists on functioning without being plugged in. Even if it could be used for storage or something, that's not what it was designed for." He shook his head. "We're all selfish, but we're not all rational."

I pondered the two perspectives. My fathers agreed, but for somewhat different reasons. John accentuated the positive: "Capitalism supports the individual." Dad took the negative approach: "Reality mandates Socialism's downfall."

Capitalism is built on incentives that reward the rationally selfish and redirect all others. In Collectivism, all the incentives rest with the Collective and none with the individual. Collectivism thrives when individuals do not act in their own self-interest, but for the ultimate benefit of others.

Without the sustained determination to put others' lives above one's own, Socialism deteriorates. Left to people's nature to pursue their own self-interest, Socialism crumbles. Because individuals will follow a course that is contrary to Socialism's success, decisions in the collective interest must be dictated and enforced centrally. It is simply a slippery slope. And Ayn Rand's personal family history shows the results. She watched Soviet Russia remove individual incentives, concentrate Power, control the means of production, and redistribute wealth. These actions ignore human nature and lead to fascism. Fascism is inconsistent with both Objectivism and Christianity.

Objections

*Many forms of government have been tried, and will be tried
in this world of sin and woe. No one pretends that democracy is
perfect or all-wise. Indeed, it has been said that democracy is the*

*worst form of government except all those other forms that have
been tried from time to time.*[14]

—Winston Churchill

Both fathers raised me to be the diehard Capitalist that I am, but I am not
entirely comfortable with either of their economic perspectives. Capitalism
feels like what Churchill said about democracy.

I listened and explored. Both see shortcomings in Capitalism (every
form of political economics has them) but not the same shortcomings.
Inconsistencies breed dilemmas, and I worked through them with my
fathers.

I understood the consistency between Capitalism and Christianity, in
part, but Dad was emphatic. "Christianity is the only religion that recognizes that men will always act in a selfish manner," he said. "It makes sense
to construct a system that will work given the reality of man's nature. Any
political or economic system that denies the reality of man's selfishness will
be frustrated." Of course, Objectivism makes the statement differently.

*Historically, capitalism worked brilliantly, and it is the only
system that will work. Socialism in every variant has led to disaster
and will again whenever it is tried. Yet socialism is admired by
mankind's teachers, while capitalism is damned.*

*The source of this inversion is the fact that freedom is selfish,
rights are selfish, capitalism is selfish.*

*It is true that freedom, rights, and capitalism are selfish. It is
also true that selfishness, properly defined, is the good.*[15]

—Leonard Peikoff

"There's a big difference between believing that humans are steeped
in sin, and are innately rebellious, and seeing selfishness as a virtue," John
said. "Thinking is not an automatic activity. It requires an act of the will.
Selfishness is a rational conclusion, but it's not a given."

I continued to challenge Dad's Christian Faith. He may have concluded in favor of Capitalism, but Christian beliefs seemed less of a solid foundation for it. Christianity seemed a lot like Socialism, where the needs of others are put above the needs of the individual. What's the difference between "from each according to his ability, to each according to his need" and "He who has two coats, let him share with him who has none."?

"The most crucial difference is choice," Dad answered. "One is voluntary based on motivations that are specific to an individual, and calls on him to choose. If it's genuine, the choice is not out of a sense of duty or compulsion; it's from the heart. The other is administered by the government, and by force of law."

Sometimes I just like pushing John's buttons. He knows where I stand, but it just sets him off. I'll throw out a hypothetical, and watch him launch into a diatribe, purely for the entertainment value. "Doesn't a capitalist system under Objectivism support shysters like Bernie Madoff?" Capitalism gets painted with a very broad brush, and I know "Wall Street" has become a pejorative euphemism for everything that is wrong with the world, from poverty to global warming. When Bernard Madoff was charged with perpetrating a Ponzi scheme in excess of $50 billion in fraud, people blamed Capitalism.

"Don't let anyone package-deal Capitalism with the actions of criminals. Capitalism recognizes individual rights. Madoff was just a criminal; there was no genius in what he did. He took money from people under false pretenses. It's never proper to exercise uninitiated force, and that's effectively what he did." In Rand's view, this kind of criminal activity set the stage for the proper purpose of any government: "to make social existence possible to men, by protecting the benefits and combating the evils which men can cause to one another."[16]

A unilateral breach of contract involves an indirect use of physical force: it consists, in essence, of one man receiving the

material values, goods or services of another, then refusing to pay
for them and thus keeping them by force (by mere physical posses-
sion), not by right—i.e., keeping them without the consent of their
owner. Fraud involves a similarly indirect use of force: it consists
of obtaining material values without their owner's consent, under
false pretenses or false promises.[17]

Dad's answer took the Conversation in the same direction. It was almost as if their passion was one and the same, but in different parts of the world, and from a different angle. Among the flurry of commentary and articles, Dad encountered the sentiment that we shouldn't really call Madoff's deception "sin." After all, it's really just human nature to deceive others. "Where we failed," the argument went, "is in our lack of government oversight. Regulation is the key to avoiding this kind of problem in the future."

"But the argument falls down on itself," Dad objected. "The same 'human nature' that led Madoff to defraud his victims is in a government made up of human beings! We're kidding ourselves if we think that's not trying to put a fire out with hot grease."

Conclusion

As I've noted, the age-old advice to avoid politics and religion as topics of conversation has never held up in my family. We talk almost exclusively about those subjects. Speaking with my fathers about politics continues to be a satisfying activity. Contrary to what I expected because of their fundamentally different world views, their political conclusions overlap.

The Conversation of world views between my fathers had been volatile and full of disagreement, from their views of sex to the way they spend their money. I was delighted with their agreement on Capitalism. I felt, for the first time, that my fathers could sit down together. I had been looking for ways to bring them together; the common ground of

Capitalism was a start. Not only did they agree about Capitalism, they agreed about Capitalism's adversaries: the unfavorable Gordon Gekko types that give Capitalism a bad name and the Collectivist looters of wealth who are (at best) well-intentioned, but misguided.

I was under no delusion that Dad and John were going to sit down over a cup of coffee, but their philosophical agreements gave me a greater hope. Agreement among people from disparate camps has strong implications for the hope we should feel in a free-market democracy. Furthermore, it was encouraging to think of these two profoundly influential constituencies combining their efforts! Those who fervently believe that government intervention is not the answer and that the empowerment of the individual is our best hope to flourish, can and *must* work together. Moreover, our inclination to agree allows us to put off the intentions that might divide us, not because they're unimportant, but because they're not expedient. And expediency is not merely utilitarian. It's a genuine necessity in these pivotal times. The precarious state of our capitalist democracy requires reasonable people to converse and to act without delay.

6

REASON

*It is true, that a little philosophy inclineth man's mind to
atheism; but depth in philosophy bringeth men's minds
about to religion.*[1]

— Sir Francis Bacon

There is a certain irony in approaching a chapter on Reason. After all,
Dad and John were best friends. It would have made sense for the two of
them to play out a Conversation of world views. Yet, as Pascal's famed cou-
plet tells us, "The heart has its reasons, of which reason does not know."
And so, those discussions never happened; events in their lives separated
them. As if taking on a will of its own, though, the Conversation found
a way, and inevitably, the forum became my life. I was a liaison between

Christianity and Objectivism, and between these two men. Over and over, we talked. The arguments they would have had with each other, they had with me. "Faith versus Reason" was among them.

I imagine the two philosophies as two lawyers in a courtroom, each appealing to each other for Reason. I am the jury. Dad heeds the plea for Reason through the prophet Isaiah, "Come, let us reason together." If God is calling us to reason with him, what does it say that we will not reason together with those whose distance is far less removed? Dad agrees with Ayn Rand that if Man is to survive and live as Man, he must live by his Reason. "In other words," he would say, "Reason is what differentiates humanity from animals. Reason, language, logic: they all define us. We're made in the image of God." Dad and John agreed about Reason, except of course, for the "God" part.

"Reason," John said as if reading right out of Ayn Rand, "is our only means of grasping Reality and of acquiring knowledge." In Rand's own words, she characterizes Reason like this:

> Man's mind is his basic means of survival—and of self-protection. Reason is the most selfish human faculty: it has to be used in and by a man's own mind, and its product—truth—makes him inflexible, intransigent, impervious to the power of any pack or any ruler.[2]

As an Objectivist, John boils everything down to what is rational. That does not mean for a moment that he is cold or humorless. On the contrary, his sense of humor improves his life and the lives of the people around him. Nevertheless, he is passionate to affirm that "Whatever negates, opposes, or destroys rationality or logic is evil." John Galt, the hero of *Atlas Shrugged*, urges his hearers to think:

> Do not say that you're afraid to trust your mind because you know so little. Live and act within the limit of your knowledge and keep expanding it to the limit of your life.[3]

John believes what Ayn Rand said about knowledge, that to know any-thing, an individual must use his mind, not emotion or intuition or, cer-tainly, not Faith. "Reason is the only way," he says. "Since Aristotle, there has not been a stronger advocate of Reason than Ayn Rand." Her philos-ophy is comprehensive, a testimony to her own Reason. Her logical argu-ments are tight and thorough.

Dad and John agree on the primacy of Reason; yet they begin at different places to get there because of their presuppositions. John's first principle is that "the universe is everything that exists, all there is." He means the nat-ural—not the supernatural—uni-verse, because the Objectivist does not recognize anything ethereal

No concept man forms is valid unless he integrates it without contradiction into the total sum of his knowledge. To arrive at a contradiction is to confess an error in one's thinking; to maintain a contradiction is to abdicate one's mind and to evict oneself from the realm of reality.[4]

—Ayn Rand

or immaterial in the supernatural sense. "Yes, emotions are ethereal," he said, "but emotions exist apart from anything supernatural." As an example, angels are supernatural by definition. They don't exist.

Thinking is the opposite of going through life without asking ques-tions. Ayn Rand's description of not thinking is "not using our mind to reason, to survive, to create for ourselves what we need to thrive." It fol-lows that a "true Objectivist" accepts no conclusion at face value, even if it comes from Rand herself. He wrestles through, thinks through, each one. Now, John is my poster boy for Objectivism; and regardless if her critics caricature Rand's followers as cultists, John gives them no reason to. On the contrary, he does not blindly follow her dictates as some sacred doc-trine. That would be to negate the very process she advocates through her philosophy. Instead, as an individual guided by Reason, he asks questions about the derivation and application of Rand's conclusions. Moreover, it's not enough to "think right." Ultimately, we want to live right. That requires living in accordance with right thinking.

If Reason is all there is, if the rational is primal, then what is Reason? What is it for, and how does it work?

> *Rationality is the recognition of the fact that existence exists, that nothing can alter the truth and nothing can take precedence over ... thinking—that the mind is one's only judge of values and one's only guide of action—that reason is an absolute that permits no compromise... the alleged short-cut to knowledge, which is faith, is only a short-circuit destroying the mind.[5]*

— John Galt

Reason suits the natural world. For the Objectivist, the natural world is all there is, so Reason is all we need.

Ayn Rand champions a life of the mind. Objectivism claims Reason as its talisman and rational self-interest as its creed. In a different way, Christians also appeal to Reason. However, Reason itself dictates that the exclusive claims of each world view cannot both be true. John rejects Faith as arbitrary whim, while Dad embraces a spiritual dimension to Reality that picks up where Reason leaves off.

This spiritual dimension is Dad's presupposition, his starting place. Contrary to the characterization that Faith is an "alleged short-cut to knowledge," the Christian maintains that Faith informs and expands knowledge. Christians see the Divine testimony behind the very existence of Reason. The argument goes something like this: "Order and logic exist; they are the building blocks of Reason. In a closed system, order does not come out of disorder. Since order and logic exist, the universe must not be a closed system. Therefore, something outside the material order of things must be at work."

Dad opened his well-worn Bible to the Old Testament book of Proverbs. "Reason is personified all through the book," he said. He showed me how the ancient writer used literary personifications of Reason: "Clear Thinking" and "Common Sense," and then went on, "The writer of Proverbs urges us not to lose sight of these companions for a minute. Before he moves to specifics, he tells us why we should care about the principles of Reason and the fruits of logic.

> *...they will be life for you,*
> *an ornament to grace your neck.*
> *Then you will go on your way in safety,*
> *and your foot will not stumble;*
> *when you lie down, you will not be afraid;*
> *when you lie down, your sleep will be sweet.*
> *Have no fear of sudden disaster*
> *or of the ruin that overtakes the wicked,*
> *for the Lord will be your confidence*
> *and will keep your foot from being snared.*
> — Proverbs 3:22-26 (NIV)

The last verse of the passage links Reason to its thematic cause. Reason keeps our souls alive and well, fit and attractive, with energy and stability and free of panic precisely because God is with us, keeping us safe and sound. Reason, Common Sense, and Clear Thinking all point to—even escort us to—God. How ironically Randian!

Reason, Common Sense, and Clear Thinking all point to— even escort us to—God. How ironically Randian!

It may not go without saying that Rand's contemporaries in the Christian community burnish the same type of argument that Rand does concerning the fundamental validity of Reason. In his 1947 book about the supernatural, C. S. Lewis wrote about Reason this way:

It follows that no account of the universe can be true unless that account leaves it possible for our thinking to be a real insight. A theory which explained everything else in the whole universe but which made it impossible to believe that our thinking was valid, would be utterly out of court. For that theory would itself have been reached by thinking, and if thinking is not valid that theory would, of course, be itself demolished. It would have destroyed its own credentials. It would be an argument which proved that no argument was sound—a proof that there are no such things as proofs—which is nonsense. [6]

Continuing from the assertion that thinking itself is necessarily valid, Lewis proceeds to argue for axioms, for the methodology of argumentation, in a similar manner as Leonard Peikoff in *Objectivism: The Philosophy of Ayn Rand.* Lewis remarks,

We know about [heredity, the struggle for existence, and elimination] only by inference. Unless, therefore, you start by assuming inference to be valid, you cannot know about them. You have to assume that inference is valid before you can even begin your argument for its validity. And a proof which sets out by assuming the thing you have to prove, is rubbish.[7]

Standing in a long tradition of Christian rationalism, Lewis is affirming what Rand would also affirm. The mechanisms of right thinking are rudimentary to the good and right living of humanity.

Furthermore, in addition to how we reason, Rand and Lewis agree on the process of reasoning. We acquire knowledge through the use of the mind. When we observe with our senses, we create a picture of the world by integrating our perceptions of Reality. Reason takes concretes and conceptualizes them into abstractions; and as we use our mind to think through what we encounter and integrate, we survive. When we do that well, we thrive. That description may seem obvious, but each of these thinkers was arguing against no less of a philosophical giant than Immanuel Kant. By Kant's reasoning, we cannot know anything for sure. But Rand agrees with Lewis when she rightly points out the extreme in Kant's faulty reasoning. He essentially claims that our faculties are flawed, and therefore we cannot trust them. Yet, without our faculties, how can we trust anything? Of course, no one lives that way. People make decisions every moment of the day that require reliance on our senses. On a dry, sunny day, I see the road ahead of me is clear and I drive straight for miles. But, at night on a windy road, I would be foolish to drive at the same speed.

My father and my stepfather would fully concur with this line of thinking. Their world views would line up to this point. However, for the Naturalist, this is the sum total of the schema by which Reason leads to knowledge. Where John the Naturalist stops, Dad the Supernaturalist keeps going. And this is where the Conversation inevitably hits a huge roadblock.

Faith

John's rationalism explicitly rejects anything that entails "blind acceptance of a certain ideational content."[8] The term Rand uses to describe this action is "faith," and to her, Faith is "wishful thinking." In her chapter entitled, "Faith and Force: The Destroyers of the Modern World,"[9] Rand shows how Reason and Freedom are the only two causes of the progress of the nineteenth century. She says that their antagonists are Faith and Force. Like Reason and Freedom, Rand says, Faith and Force go together. I didn't think about Force very much, despite my frequent episodes of pounding—and getting pounded—on the wrestling mat. For some reason, though, Faith seemed compelling to me, and I wanted to understand both my fathers' perspectives.

John treats Faith as the opposite of Reason. "Faith" in John's vocabulary means trusting something that any thinking person could not trust. "Are you kiddin' me?" he says with DeNiro-esque flair. "My life would be so much easier! If I could, I would." His comments stop short of adding, "If I could just check my brain at the door, I would be like one of those Christians, leading a life of spiritual devotion." Likewise, many Objectivists might articulate Christian Faith similarly as the sentiment that helps a person convince himself that the object is blue, even though his Reason tells him it's red. What I was coming to learn was that the essence of Faith is one of the biggest misunderstandings that Objectivists—and sometimes Christians—have regarding Christianity. But, as my Dad would assert, the Christian sees Faith as discerning what God wants to do. Many times, this will even be in the absence of empirical proof, but to the believer, substantive and real nonetheless.

"Faith complements and completes Reason, not the other way around." Dad honestly does not believe that the two are at odds. He would be quick to point out that "the opposite of Reason is actually *irrationality*. And depending on how you look at it, the opposite of Faith is either Unbelief or 'Works.'" It is popular to accept the definition of Faith as the absence of Reason, and I certainly had conceived it as such. But Dad pointed out to me that the Bible itself offers several tests, identifying the dangers of merely blind faith (much less the kind of "wishful thinking" Rand thought it was), rather than lifting Faith up as the highest virtue. He gave me an example from the Old and New Testament: "If what a prophet proclaims in the name of the Lord does not take place or come true, that is a message the Lord has not spoken."[10] Then there's also the Apostle Paul's simple exhortation: "Test everything. Hold on to the good."[11]

"You see," Dad said, "the Bible does not exempt itself from its own criteria of truth. It does not hold up the abdication of Reason—the annihilation of the mind—as the means to know God."

I braced myself for the impassioned words that were coming. For my farmer father, second only to defending the Gospel was defending the rationality of Christian thought. If you were to meet him, with his oil-stained, dirt-worn overalls and the meaty hands of a man who actually works with them, you might never guess what a man of the mind he is. In fact, Dad is a brilliant problem-solver and a critical thinker. He achieved a master's and doctorate, founded and built three businesses, operated a small farm, and raised my younger brother as a single parent. As a matter of fact, if she could witness Dad solving problems on the farm, Ayn Rand herself would applaud his commitment to Reason as man's means of survival. Where Rand would be appalled, however, was precisely where Dad was going now, to his emphatic explanation of Biblical rationalism.

"Scripture underscores the importance of the rational, physical, and concrete as a means for knowing God. To believe something ONLY because someone else tells you to is not Faith, but mindlessness. But to believe something from a source that has proven trustworthy in the past requires both Reason and Faith."

I used to look at him quite skeptically when he coupled these ideas; but I had come to know how to lay out the argument myself: Reason is required to determine the dependability of the source, based on concrete examples of consistent truthfulness. Faith, because a record of dependability can never fully erase the doubt in our minds. We realize (rationally, by our human experience) that past truthfulness is not necessarily a guarantee of future reliability. Therefore, Faith involves both an acceptance of a past reliability (tested by Reason), as well as a belief that such reliability will continue into the future.

Dad continued. "When I say that I have 'faith' in something, I mean that I am prepared to believe that it is true based on a rational consideration of the evidence available to me, rather than requiring explicit logical or physical proof of whatever it is that I'm considering. Once I acquire proof, my faith in something becomes knowledge instead."

Another example made Dad's description more concrete for me. I have faith that the country of France exists, because I have a large body of evidence upon which to base my belief in France, even though I have no actual proof that it exists (i.e., I've never been there). I have books that describe this "France," eyewitness accounts that I am prepared to accept as accurate, a documented language and history of such a place, etc. So I have faith that if I were to hop a plane to France I'd be standing in front of the Eiffel Tower within a few hours. But unless and until I actually do that, I have no actual proof that there is, in reality, such a place, or such a tower.

Faith, as I had always understood it, involved rejecting one's rational faculty, something I was not about to do. We use our rational faculty on a daily basis to make the decisions and judgments required to live in this world, and many of those decisions and judgments are based on a reasonable and rational consideration of evidence rather than any logical or physical proof of the bases of our decisions.

Faith in the existence of France, however, does not require a rejection of rationality. Otherwise, why would an Objectivist ever set out on a journey to France (or to New Jersey, or anyplace else) for the first time, unless he had "faith" that what he was seeking lay at the end of that journey? Just because someone says "Yeah, sure, I've been to France; it's great, you should go," doesn't mean that France is actually there. They could be insane or lying.

So, whether we acknowledge it or not, every individual is a person of Faith.

Without faith, we would be paralyzed. We believe that all men are created equal; that our mothers, or at least our dogs, love us; that the #4 bus will eventually come. All these represent a belief in the unseen. The question is not then, 'Are we people of faith?'

which we as a species seem to be. But rather, 'What then is the
nature of that faith and what actions does it lead to?[12]

— Mary Gordon

It's also worth pointing out that Faith applies to relationships in the same way. Our knowledge of another person is limited, because our Reason can only be based on what *we* observe. That's a lot, but there's more to Reality than what an individual can take in. There are certain aspects of a person that exceed our capacity to understand, because human beings are complex. For example, we may observe a person's behavior, reasonably assess his probable intentions, and be entirely wrong without any proof to the contrary!

No one observes Reality omnisciently. John does not purport to do so; neither, it seems, does Rand. More likely, the second of the two alternatives follows her line of reasoning. Namely, what we observe about a person is all that matters in valuing him. If what we see is all there is, and what we see leads us to the conclusion that the person is a "moocher," there's really no more to discuss. If there is more to a person than what we observe—if the value is hidden—then perhaps our conclusions are wrong. The fact is that the value of a person or the true nature of a circumstance often remains unclear to us until it is revealed. That revelation may be independent of my rational faculties.

Revelation

Even as I came to understand aspects of Reason and Faith interlinking, I also came to understand that there were other aspects of Faith that utterly seem to belie Reason. Rand would have scoffed, for example, at Eugene Peterson's characterization of Faith.

Faith designates a way of life that takes place in an inti-
mate web of visible and invisible, silence and speech, light and

darkness, chaos and cosmos, knowledge and mystery, God and us. It is far too complex to explicitly define or explain. And since all the dimensions and elements are re-configured uniquely in each human soul, there is no immediate model that can be copied or followed.[13]

In other words, inherent in the way of Faith is a process of revelation, of having the very reality of Faith revealed to us. Admittedly, Faith doesn't sound concrete. It seems airy and subjective. Peterson goes on to say that Faith

> *...cannot be learned by copying, not by imitating, not by mastering some "faith-skills." We are all originals when we live by faith.*
>
> *But "faith" is not commonly used in this hard-traveling way. More often it is clichéd into a feeling or fantasy or disposition—a kind of wish upwards, an inclination indistinguishable from a whim and easily dissipated by a gust of wind or the distraction of a pretty face.*[14]

More thorough arguments have been made, but to get the gist of the reasoning that leads a Christian to revelation as a source of Knowledge, consider the steps that follow. Jesus's teaching was filled with references to the authority of Hebrew Scripture. His claims of Scriptural authority, as well as his claims to his own supernatural authority could be false, in whole or in part. If Jesus's death is truly the end of the story, then I have good reason to disregard his claims and authority. On the other hand, if Jesus did rise from the dead as he said he would, then everything else he said receives a seal of validation, and I have to reexamine everything in light of his resurrection.

> *The great Lord Jesus came from outside and voluntarily and deliberately attached himself to the Old Testament, affirmed it to*

be the word of God and set himself, at cost, to fulfill it. This fact of facts cuts the ground from under any suspicion that the doctrine of biblical authority rests on a circular argument such as, 'I believe the Bible to be authoritative because the Bible says it is authoritative.' Not so! It was Jesus who came 'from outside' as the incarnate Son of God, Jesus who was raised from the dead as the Son of God with power, who chose to validate the Old Testament in retrospect and the New Testament in prospect, and who is himself the grand theme of the 'story-line' of both Testaments, the focal-point giving coherence to the total 'picture' in all its complexities.[15]

— J. A. Motyer

In the reasoning of the Christian, the resurrection figures centrally. Paul the Apostle says "And if Christ weren't raised, then all you're doing is wandering about in the dark, as lost as ever. It's even worse for those who died hoping in Christ and resurrection, because they're already in their graves. If all we get out of Christ is a little inspiration for a few short years, we're a pretty sorry lot."[16] If you ever want to use logic to shut up a Christian, simply try to disprove the resurrection using valid rules of evidence. The whole of Christian reasoning hangs on it.

A Blasphemous Twist?

The methodology drilled into me by my mother and stepfather, it turns out, was precisely the skill that equipped me to consider the claims of Jesus and the Bible. While John lectured, Mom redirected the discussion to the practical: how my world view impacts my thinking when I wake up, how right thinking makes you a better person, how I shouldn't just take something at face value; I should question, and work hard to get to the truth. Not academic truth so much, but hard common sense Truth: the stuff that's so solid you can hold onto it and it'll stand the test of life's ups and downs.

III

I don't think she ever considered that by digging deep and seeking hard after Truth, I would come to a different conclusion than she did (parents beware!). Several years later, continuing my pursuit of Truth—digging deeper and all that—having survived cancer and radiation therapy, I began to consider Jesus Christ.

My biggest fear was that at the end of my life I would be on my deathbed saying, "I spent my life on the wrong thing." And, I would have no excuse, because all my life I had been taught to reason, dig, pursue, and persevere until you find what's true, and then keep going higher up and deeper in. If Jesus is where Truth is found, I had to investigate or risk missing out. G. K. Chesterton said, "Christianity has not been tried and found wanting; it has been found difficult and not tried."

That was over twenty-five years ago, and it was one of my many beginnings. I have been on the journey ever since. Despite having no substantial church background to speak of, I jumped in. I looked, I poked and asked questions, not always in the Randian fashion, but in a way that was characterized by Reason, practicality, and common sense. I don't think I will ever stop asking questions—I haven't so far—and I apply Ayn Rand's process of thought to everything.

I wonder who would think it more blasphemous, an Objectivist or a Christian, that Ayn Rand led me to Christ. But, it's true; and for that I will forever be grateful.

7

MEANING

"The philosophers of the past were superficial," Dr. Pritchett went on. "It remained for our century to redefine the purpose of philosophy. The purpose of philosophy is not to help men find the meaning of life, but to prove to them that there isn't any."[1]

— Dr. Simon Pritchett, Philosopher

He has made everything beautiful in its time. He has also set eternity in the human heart; yet no one can fathom what God has done from beginning to end.[2]

— King Solomon

Men go abroad to wonder at the heights of mountains, at
the huge waves of the sea, at the long courses of the rivers,
at the vast compass of the ocean, at the circular motions of
the stars, and they pass by themselves without wondering.[3]

— Augustine

There is nothing quite like a life-threatening disease following on the heels of an identity-threatening family crisis to dislodge a torrent of questions about Meaning in life. Let those events blow into the storm of adolescence and, well, that's what they call the "perfect storm." What prepared me for that tempest, and what I am earnestly grateful for, was my fathers' genuine commitment to the integrity of Meaning in their lives. Plenty of people don't have that. Plenty of people go about from day to day, mindlessly living, "without wondering" as Augustine wrote, with no consideration of Meaning. But as my discussions with my fathers evidenced richly, we need know what gives us Meaning. We need to know to live well.

Dad and John have different ideas about life's Meaning. By John's standard, Dad never seemed to live well. I can see his point. "But, to each his own, right?" John would say. All his life, Dad has been attached to a particular one hundred fifty acres near the Mississippi River, somewhere between St. Louis and Hannibal, Missouri. The place he reserves in his heart for nostalgia is where he forges the chains that bind him to the farm, out of loyalty and a sense of heritage. Dad moved around a lot growing up. As the son of an itinerant minister, his life was a cross between that of a "missionary kid" and a "military brat." He learned to hold in his frustration and make the best of every situation. Being a pastor's son became the "calling" that was thrust upon him. He didn't choose that calling. He didn't choose the instability of moving every two years. But it was his nonetheless. I always thought that his inordinate desire for roots was inevitable. That was the overwhelming desire through which he filtered every decision.

Dad's Great Uncle Marion owned the farm before him, and he commanded a hefty purchase price. The amount of debt required to operate the farm created such a burden that the bank repossessed Dad's machinery and nearly took the property. All of this left very little to live on, let alone "live well." I was quiet about it, but my unavoidable conclusions had to be obvious to both Dad and John. As far as I could tell, if living well related to material comfort and success, Dad's life was short on Meaning.

John lived well. Unlike my dad's family, John's stayed put; but he grew up with struggles of his own. His father came from Italy at the age of sixteen, and made his way in the garment business. He found an entrepreneurial niche, first in New York, and then in South Philadelphia, where he raised a family in a row house on Wolf and Mildred streets. John's family and neighbors created a strong, Italian identity, and his proud father and warm, supporting mother enabled him to thrive with many fewer material comforts than I enjoyed under his roof as a boy.

When John made his first million, he began modifying his lifestyle in a manner that revealed his longstanding aspirations. Though I have never seen an actual "list," John's accomplishments and accoutrements read like the wish list of a lottery winner. If he had written a letter to the Cosmic Santa, who passes out grown-up toys for good adults, it would have listed the material elements of his world that define living well. He owned a plane (not to mention an entire airline), race horses (along with a horse farm in Florida), a second home on the ocean, a pinball machine, and a '53 Ford Victoria with a flathead V-8 engine, chrome bumpers, and original pink paint. As the son of the woman he loved—and for no other reason—I was allowed to partake in this life well lived. I felt unworthy, fortunate, sometimes guilty, but nevertheless grateful.

It is Rand's fictional and real-life villains who believe life is meaningless; Rand believes life *has* Meaning. Some of her detractors see philosophy as a tool to prove that life is meaningless. She says philosophy's function is to help us know life's purpose. John has always communicated that there is no higher value than my own life, because without my life, I cannot assess or understand values. But survival is not enough. It's not just living that drives us as humans, but living to the maximum human potential. The real end of life, the highest purpose, is to live well. A flourishing life is a good and proper life, a truly human life based on potentialities or capacities that are intrinsic to man's nature. A plant is flourishing when it is strong, healthy, and capable of living. Health and strength not only stave off death in the moment, but raise the chances of survival in the future. The "good life" is one that sustains itself and enhances its own vitality.

When Dagny Taggart first lands in Galt's Gulch, she finds a place to which the producers of the world have defected to in order to live a life of rational self-interest. She finds, to her amazement, a perpetual energy machine created by John Galt. Her response illustrates what makes her tick. An individual achieves happiness, in her estimation, through production, which enhances the quality of life. For Dagny, the motor in Galt's Gulch is the embodiment of human productive capacity. It is "the power of an incomparable mind given shape in a net of wires sparkling peacefully under a summer sky, drawing an incalculable power out of space into the secret interior of a small stone hovel."[4]

> But she knew that there was no meaning in motors or factories or trains, that their only meaning was in man's enjoyment of his life, which they served—and that her swelling admiration at the sight of an achievement was for the man from whom it came, for the power and the radiant vision within him which had seen the earth as a place of enjoyment and had known that the work of achieving one's happiness was the purpose, the sanction and the meaning of life.[5]

Achieving happiness is her only goal and the sole purpose of her activities. To enhance her life, she produces. Dagny is not an isolated, robotic creature. She is inspired and enriched by the productivity and excellence of others' labors as well. Dagny's productiveness achieved life's Meaning and purpose.

In contrast, Rand speaks of the man who is devoid of Meaning. She describes "the man whom people call practical."

> ...the man who despises principles, abstractions, art, philosophy and his own mind. He regards the acquisition of material objects as the only goal of existence—and he laughs at the need to consider their purpose or their source. He expects them to give him pleasure—and he wonders why the more he gets, the less he feels.[6]

I was curious about what made Dagny thrive. "Does her happiness ever go beyond what she produces?" I asked John. "Are the values that sustain and enhance her life strictly material values?"

"It's not just material values that sustain and enhance your life; nonmaterial values too," John spoke quickly to prevent me from jumping to a conclusion. "Make no mistake," he said. "Meaning is linked to my achievement. My end—what keeps me going, my purpose—is making my life better. I produce and accumulate for my own happiness; that is the purpose of my life." Then he repeated John Galt's oath:

> I swear by my life and my love of it that I will never live for the sake of another man, nor ask another man to live for mine.[7]

I knew what he meant. While his life's Meaning was centered on himself, it wasn't devoid of non-material values. He made room for love, relationships, and beauty: ethereal aspects of human existence. All of these things were meaningful to John, but it wasn't what I thought of as Meaning. I thought of Meaning as something that would last. Something that, in the grander scheme, would make an impact: an enduring legacy. If the universe is all there is, and we believe that everything we have built will die, then there is no true Meaning beyond what is temporal and fleeting. Was I onto something? Or were these thoughts simply another way of responding to my near-death experiences?

Ayn Rand concludes that some people lead lives of flourishing and others do not. With productiveness as the standard, some people's lives will always be more "meaningful" than others'. Of course, each individual's life is meaningful to that individual. More than that, one person's production accrues to another.

For example, I never met the founder of Apple, Steve Jobs. I derive benefit from his innovation. My life flourishes because of his production. True, he made a huge amount of money, enjoyed more material comforts than I do, but his benefit stems from his ability to produce. I benefited from Steve Jobs' production by means of trade, but I benefited from John's production because I am the son of the woman he loves.

So, if the purpose of life is to live it well, and some are living it better than others, then they are achieving life's purpose to a greater degree. There is no eternal destiny or ethereal purpose, Rand says, beyond the individual's life. People are not eternal beings; nothing exists beyond the grave. Does Rand say that we should "eat, drink, and be merry, for tomorrow we die." No, she does not. Instead, we should understand and live according to our nature as human beings. We are rational beings, and as such, we are to live in a manner according to that nature. That means that we should strive for the balance that will lead to the most flourishing.

Meaning and Personhood

Dad and John both want meaningful lives. I guess everyone does. Furthermore, they generally agree on the attributes of that life, the specifics of which the good life consists. However, Dad's conception of Meaning is rooted deep in the Christian understanding of Man created in the Image of God. "God, the Great 'I AM,' is a Person; so we are all persons." Dad went on. "The idea of personhood is unique to human beings." Ayn Rand does validate personhood, but she places considerably less emphasis on relationships between persons, and she certainly attributes none of that identity to an Almighty Creator.

In Ayn Rand's *Anthem*, civilization has reverted to an existence without science and technology. In this world, Altruism and Collectivism are the reigning philosophies, and everyone exists solely for the sake of the greater society. When I shared the story with Dad, he told me about C. S. Lewis and Charles Williams, who both pictured a Hell where you could no longer utter the holy word, "I." According to these authors, Hell is where one has lost his "self." Lewis' own friend and contemporary, J.R.R. Tolkien paints a vivid picture of this in the character of Golem. He is the 'un-man,' the one who loses self. In *The Lord of the Rings*, Golem no longer says, "I." He speaks of himself in the third person. This loss of the "I" as a particular identity, created and ordained to exist by God Himself, is a distortion. Although the opposite, the aggrandizement of self, is an equally erroneous distortion, Christians have a tendency to react against assertions of the self. Dad characterized this as being "underawed" by the beauty of God's creation, having created us in His own image. The danger of being underawed is to miss the authentic or real person God intended each of us to be. Ironically, this anemic view of personhood, even in the name of piety, has all the trappings of idolatry.

As for Golem, he is no longer precious to himself; rather, he has become a slave to the "Precious," the ring he seeks to possess. In the psychology of damnation, we lose ourselves when we make a god, an idol, of anything other than God. Only when I recognize God's definition of Reality—the Meaning behind who I am as a person—am I truly ready to experience myself authentically. When I unpack that idea, I'm compelled to consider the "idols" in my own life.

Some of the best years of my life were in Manhattan. My wife and I moved there when we our boys were still in diapers, and we stayed after business school. When a recession hit, I lost my position and we had to move. Several years later, I still feel like a New Yorker in exile: Exile being the operative word. There are times when it physically aches to be away from the City. It took me years to stop choking on the name of another city when I told anyone where I lived.

At a distance, I see that New York City attracted me for more than just its culture, activity, and sophistication. Living there, I connected to something bigger than myself; the attraction was strong. City living was certainly no less than an adventure. While my work was not exactly a cause, Manhattan was a living organism, and I was part of it, living inside it. New York is a world-class city, and I thrived on the energy pulsating through it.

My friend Tim thinks that my description of the withdrawal I suffered leaving New York (and still feel) is actually an identity issue: what he calls, "an idol of the heart." There's a sense that my attachment to New York City has gone beyond finding Meaning. It has worked itself into my identity. In other words, when I think of myself as a New Yorker, part of that living organism, I can rest easy. I validate myself based on belonging to something bigger than myself.

Tim's words stay with me. His reference to "an idol" pictures the first of the Ten Commandments:

> *You shall not make for yourself an image in the form of any-thing in heaven above or on the earth beneath or in the waters below. You shall not bow down to them or worship them.*
> — Deuteronomy 5:8-9 (NIV)

If anything defines who I am, it is a god to me. It determines whether or not I receive life with joy and contentment. Being a New Yorker shaped my identity and leaving New York challenged my ability to be either joyful or content.

We tend to think of idols as patently bad things—addiction, obsession, dogmatism. But just as often, it's a patently *good* thing that we give too much power to in our hearts. I place a high value on fatherhood. I wanted to be a great father for my sons, to be nurturing, strong, and stable for them. Being a good father was important to me, from the moment they were born; and watching them grow, I lived to be a good dad. But there were some dysfunctions about my parenting that stemmed from finding *too* much of my worth in my role as a father. It became much more than what it seemed at first. It became an idol. When my sons were doing well, I felt good about life. I felt at ease and could accept life with happiness and peace. When they were struggling, not only was I struggling more than they, but I was struggling to see that I was worth anything at all as a person, let alone respond to life with poise. Instead of being their stable rock of a dad, I threw the weight of my soul on my role as a father. And it buckled.

Søren Kierkegaard's basic argument in *Sickness Unto Death* is that despair (the sickness unto death) is a sickness of the self, a "self-disorder." My various forms of idolatry are just that, a disorder unto despair. Kierkegaard's expression of despair comes in three flavors, each form expressing a wrong relationship to the "self." In Kierkegaard's first two forms of despair, the individual is unable to recognize or experience who he really is, or his "self." In *Anthem*, Ayn Rand demonstrates her agreement with the first two of these aspects of despair because her characters are forbidden to be individuals in their society, or even to use the word "I". The results are disastrous. Kierkegaard's third definition, however, gives Objectivists headaches. In describing Kierkegaard's definition, Timothy Keller says,

> *Sin is despairing refusal to find your deepest identity in your relationship and service to God. Sin is seeking to become oneself, to get an identity, apart from him. Everyone gets their*

identity, their sense of being distinct and valuable, from some-
where or something. Kierkegaard asserts that human beings were
not made only to believe in God in some general way, but to love
him supremely, center their lives on him above anything else, and
build their very identities on him. Anything other than that is sin.[8]

I certainly understand what he is describing. On any given day, I may
be building my identity apart from Jesus Christ. On any given day, I may
be enmeshed in a funk of living three hours from New York. Two of my
favorite movies of all time include heroes who likewise look for their identity somewhere apart from God. Rocky is ultimately successful, but "not
being a bum" is the motivation that drives his existence.

All I wanna do is go the distance. Nobody's ever gone the
distance with Creed, and if I can go that distance, you see, and
that bell rings and I'm still standin', I'm gonna know for the
first time in my life, see, that I weren't just another bum from
the neighborhood.[9]

Harold Abrahams, an Olympic runner in *Chariots of Fire*, said it this way:

I'm forever in pursuit and I don't even know what I am chasing.
And now in one hour's time, I will be out there again. I will
raise my eyes and look down that corridor; four feet wide, with ten
lonely seconds to justify my existence. But will I?[10]

At particular points in my life, I have sought to "justify my existence"
variously. I have been defined by academic performance, career success, my
salary, parental approval, the approval of my peers, being a good father, and
being a good husband. I am convinced that these are all good things. But
they cannot sustain my identity; neither were they meant to. Even when
I achieve the full measure of success in these areas, a longing remains for
something more permanent. Matthew Arnold captures a sense of mystery

which both Christianity and Objectivism attempt to dispel in their respective ways.

> *But often, in the world's most crowded streets,*
> *But often, in the din of strife,*
> *There rises an unspeakable desire*
> *After the knowledge of our buried life:*
> *A thirst to spend our fire and restless force*
> *In tracking out our true, original course;*
> *A longing to inquire*
> *Into the mystery of this heart which beats*
> *So wild, so deep in us—to know*
> *Whence our lives come and where they go.*[11]

Christianity recognizes the longing. Christians find, in Christ, the answer to their deepest desires. Objectivism, on the other hand, identifies the longing, but disposes of it differently. At worst, it is a fabrication of the individual's consciousness. It is, at best, an individual's aspiration to achieve.

> *"Dagny, there's nothing of any importance in life—except how well you do your work. Nothing. Only that. Whatever else you are, will come from that. It's the only measure of human value... When you grow up, you'll know what I mean."*
> *"I know it now. But ... Francisco, why are you and I the only ones who seem to know it?"*[12]

[Work] "is the only measure of human value... When you grow up, you'll know what I mean."

Historically, philosophy takes one of two perspectives on Meaning. Nigel Warburton implies that Meaning can come from God, or it can come from inside the individual.

> *If God exists, then human existence may have a purpose, and we may even hope for eternal life. If not, then we must create any*

meaning in our lives for ourselves: no meaning will be given to them from outside, and death is probably final.[13]

His view has certainly been the predominant view for many years. On the one hand you've got God, the Meaning-giver, and on the other, subjective, relative meaning. Some emerging philosophical views even bypass the issue of Meaning altogether. Dennett, Dawkins, and Hitchens, the "New Atheists," all equate Meaning with what they value. If they value intelligence or beauty, their appreciation of that becomes their Meaning; and Rand would fall into the same camp.

It is certainly within the historic philosophical discussion to link the question, "Who am I?" to the question "What am I here for?" C. S. Lewis relates that his own search for Meaning led to his conversion. A lack of Meaning contributes to what Pascal called a "God-shaped void," but the longing for Meaning finds its fulfillment in God. Objectivists write this off as mystical: consciousness taking precedence over existence. Even after reading Rand's arguments to the contrary, I could not explain the deep sense of longing in each individual. The Christian sees that as God-placed.

In Lewis's attempts to articulate the longing of the human heart, he describes beauty, nostalgia, romance, and a secret intimacy that the best of our human experiences can only foreshadow. All of these are wonderful, but they only *point* to what we truly long for.

These things—the beauty, the memory of our won past—are good images of what we really desire; but if they are mistaken for the thing itself, they turn into dumb idols, breaking the hearts of their worshippers. For they are not the thing itself; they are only the scent of a flower we have not found, the echo of a tune we have not heard, news from a country we have never yet visited.[14]

Whether or not we are conscious of a desire that no natural happiness will satisfy may not be reason enough, Lewis concedes, to suppose that Reality offers anything to satisfy it. Being hungry does not prove that a man has or will get bread. "But surely," Lewis says, "a man's hunger does prove that he comes of a race which repairs its body by eating and inhabits a world where eatable substances exist."[15] He does not believe that his deep longing proves it will be satisfied. However, the very existence of the desire indicates that something exists that will, or at least could, satisfy it.

A man may love a woman and not win her; but it would be very odd if the phenomenon called 'falling in love' occurred in a sexless world.[16]

The longing in my own heart came out of the questions thrust upon me by the cancer I battled at sixteen years old. I couldn't help asking the questions that came out of my own tragedy. Why me? What was the cause of my suffering? Was there some cause outside of science? Was this related to some cosmic sense of justice visited upon me? Or the question that follows almost immediately. "Why *not* me? Why isn't it worse than I am experiencing?" Before the cancer was diagnosed, everything was up in the air. I didn't know what I had, but I knew I was still alive. I couldn't imagine going through the hell of my hospital roommate, who had a wife and children coming to visit. Either way, these questions as much as anything else in my young life compelled me to reckon with that longing, that desire to find the Meaning of my life.

Viewing Myself

Meaning comes from what you value the most, your standard of value. For the Objectivist, that's the individual. Rand emphasizes that Man's nature dictates that he survives through the use of his mind. Through the mind, we produce what we need to live. It's not surprising that Francisco and Dagny, two of Rand's heroes, agree that productive work is the measure of human value.

Furthermore, you are what the most important people in your life think you are. That goes for the Christian as well as the Objectivist. While there may be some misconceptions, neither world view says that we're supposed to look to public opinion or some community consensus to weigh in on who we are and what we're worth. The Christian says that God is the ultimate authority on that count, and postmodern thinkers react violently to this assertion of an absolute authority. Prevalent today is the assertion that an individual needs to determine his own worth, his own value, based on criteria that is personal and subjective, if not private. The Objectivist says that we must see objectively (based on the nature of Reality) that we are valuable. That value is based on our production or, perhaps, our capacity to produce.

If following a moral code leads to the goal of reaching the highest ideal for ourselves, then we will base our valuation of ourselves on how well we live up to it. If, as Rand would maintain, our ability to produce is the primary factor that accomplishes our survival and happiness, then our ability to produce becomes that standard. By Rand's criteria, those whose achievements meet a certain standard of quality have more value than those whose achievements do not. If John has value because he lives up to certain criteria, then he must esteem another person's value as lesser if they have not matched his productiveness. To him, it is not competition, merely evaluation.

Conclusion

With my investigation of Meaning, the direction of the Conversation has taken a turn. Coming to terms with a world view meant facing the emotional, intellectual, and spiritual challenges of my life thus far. Divorce, cancer, separation from a parent—these experiences certainly pushed me to make sense of the bigger picture in life. As I developed a foundational understanding of each world view, I launched into topics paramount in my own life struggles: Sex and Money. These two themes are manifestly practical, as is Capitalism, and the Conversation clarified my fathers' perspectives, since it is often easier to determine *what* people believe than why they believe it. But how do the relatively concrete "what's"—like Sex and Money—relate to Meaning? It turned out that my study of how these men understood and applied Reason to *every* aspect of their lives brought me to Meaning.

The search for Meaning has occupied many brilliant minds over the centuries. From the Academy to the dorm room, individuals have sought to comprehend the underlying purpose or Meaning of their existence. In connecting my fathers' world views to Meaning, it became clear that Dad lives to glorify God and sees Meaning as dependent on a Supreme Being. John sees existence itself as Reality. Along with Rand, he says that asking for anything else is a futile pursuit. Both men would consider their values objective, which is to say, true for everyone. The turn for me happened here. I found that John's explanation didn't satisfy, and while dissatisfaction itself didn't validate Dad's answer, I felt myself leaning in his direction. I recognized there is plenty we may value in life that is not lasting. It may be meaningful, in a temporal sense, but if it came about by chance and it fades away, there is no ultimate purpose to it. Valued aspects of life may be meaning*ful*, but this is not Meaning. I had become convinced that true, cosmic Meaning was imbued with purpose that outlives all that we know.

Along with that most unlikely of converts to Christianity, J. Gordon Liddy, it was no rush of emotion that led me to Christ, but a genuine "rush of reason."[17]

I was a Christian, but questions kept coming. The exploration of true Meaning continued. I found that there were more abstractions to lasso, more Conversations to spark. What of Power or Joy? Yet I knew that what needed tackling next was intimately close to home. In the end of the day, there is no significant investigation of Meaning in our lives without understanding something even more rudimentary, our very selves.

8

SELFISHNESS

"What's love, darling, if it's not self-sacrifice" she went on lightly, in the tone of a drawing-room discussion. "What's self-sacrifice, unless one sacrifices that which is one's most precious and most important? But I don't expect you to understand it. ... You'd let the whole world perish rather than soil that immaculate self of yours with a single spot of which you'd have to be ashamed."[1]

— Lillian Rearden, to her husband

A Visceral Response

Notwithstanding Ayn Rand's sustained popularity over the last fifty years, her vocabulary can be somewhat off-putting. "Selfishness" does not play well in today's society. If I listed Selfishness as a strength on a job application (or even as a glaring weakness) I would be politely and hurriedly shown the exit. There is a reason for that.

Most of us have met enough people to identify "the selfish person." At a glance, we see someone who draws attention to himself in almost everything he does. He wants others to know about *his* talents, *his* character, and *his* accomplishments so that *he* can be lifted up. As the old joke goes, "Enough about *me*, let's talk about *you*. What do *you* think about *me*?" Outside his own knowledge and activity, nothing else exists. I dislike the selfish person; except, of course, when I am being selfish. In fact, I tend to loathe the selfish person even more deeply when I see in him what I dislike about myself.

Selfishness Misunderstood and Defended

Rand's *The Virtue of Selfishness* is a collection of essays that first appeared in "The Objectivist Newsletter." The title alone incites criticism and disgust from many circles. But Ayn Rand was content to antagonize those who misunderstood her meaning. She identified many profound moral issues at stake. For Rand, the virtue of Selfishness is not just provocative semantics, or a clever way of drawing attention to her philosophy. It stems from the foundational building blocks of her thought: specifically, her conception of Man's highest value.

Selfishness is an Objectivist ideal, but Rand does a disservice to herself and her philosophy by leading with such a provocative and misunderstood term. If she had started with "rational self-interest" instead of Selfishness, she may have reached more individuals, but then she would not have stirred up a fuss. I think she wanted the fuss.

Ayn Rand railed against what she called Altruism: the doctrine that says, "it's a virtue if I act for your benefit, especially if it disadvantages me." A lot of people don't really understand Altruism. It's not just being nice to others; it is "Other-ism." By definition, Altruism says that everyone else is more important than you. Rand attacked self-sacrifice, but she wasn't talking about benevolence. She had this very precise idea that you shouldn't sacrifice yourself to others or others to you. In the language of our culture, Selfishness is cutting someone off in a line, or taking the last doughnut that someone else wants, behavior with rather negative connotations. You, not the Collective, own your own life. It doesn't mean that you don't help someone else in need. It means that you are the one who makes that choice. So, hearing Rand lift up Selfishness and attack Altruism sounds like an attack on goodness itself.

The Objectivist's standard of value is his own life: the "life of the individual." Without the actual, physical life of the individual, he can have no values at all; so the survival and enhancement of that life is paramount. It follows that Self comes first in everything. That's what Rand means by Selfishness. As an Objectivist, John considers his own benefit first and foremost in every one of his decisions.

Sam is a successful CEO, having run more than one company in his life. He has the uncanny ability to identify what needs to be done, articulate a plan, and mobilize the people around him. He has charisma. People want to please him and be near him. His virtues are just like Dagny's; his Selfishness also reminds me of Dagny. He might consider that a compliment, but miss the implications. Every time I visit him, he seems preoccupied, especially in his office. He overlooks the people around him. They are uninteresting, and "flat" (ironically, like Ayn Rand's characters). Through years of focusing only on his work, he alienated his family. He's divorced. His children, now adults, have suffered incalculably because of his neglect. I asked him once, in a somber moment, "If you had a 'do over,' would you do it differently?" He pondered. "You mean, would I change my course, and change my decisions?" He paused; he gave the question the thought it deserved. "I definitely have regrets. I'm not going to say I wouldn't change some things; for sure. But would I do everything differently? Would I change my priorities? Probably not."

Thinking about Sam, my first response to the heroes in Rand's novels was both attraction and repulsion. Dagny's relentless and unflappable focus on her work requires her uninterrupted attention to what she can affect in the world. She cannot affect the weather, the actions of her competitors, or the affections of the people around her. But she can and does set her mind on building a railroad: laying the track, scheduling the trains, and coordinating the workers. She does her job, and she does it well. When I picture Dagny Taggart as a potential coworker, I'm impressed with her talent; she gets things done. She's a courageous entrepreneur, proactive and intentional. That's a virtue, and I admire it.

Those familiar with Ayn Rand and her "virtue of Selfishness" mostly fall into one of two camps. Often, they are indifferent. They have not read Ayn Rand, or they dismiss her world view almost immediately. Others, like quite a few people I've seen with John, embrace Rand's world view with fond attachment, but with misunderstanding. The TV show "The Colbert Report" proved a great example of the former camp. Comedy is a powerful means to communicate ideas, since it's hard to be angry when you're laughing.

In an attempt to entertain and poke fun at Ayn Rand and her philosophy, Colbert dedicated a portion of his show on Comedy Central to *Atlas Shrugged*. His listening audience is likely without Randian inclinations; he concluded the segment with this:

I think I can speak for everyone out there advocating following the advice of a fifty-year-old novel, set in an America that never existed. That when millions are losing jobs, losing homes, and losing hope, there is nothing more important than putting yourself first.[2]

Colbert's somewhat sarcastic tone implies his conclusions are self-evident. The audience laughs as if the sheer suggestion speaks for itself. Of course, everyone knows that "putting yourself first" is ludicrous. He gets a chuckle. In his choice to mock Rand, he may miss the irony: there is clearly *something* compelling and enduring about that fifty-year-old novel. Colbert was not, after all, satirizing *Doctor Zhivago* or even Kerouac's *On the Road*, both published the same year as *Atlas Shrugged*.

Selfishness as a Virtue

In her philosophy, Rand draws from Aristotle, who assumes that "living well" applies to everyone who is living. Anything that promotes the life of the individual is a virtue. Not just the twenty-first-century American idea of creature comforts, but down to the most basic aspects of survival! Enhancing one's own life refers to one's *own* happiness, and decidedly not the happiness of others. If "happiness" is the destination, we ask "What does it mean to be happy?" and "What will make me happy?" John is convinced that human beings will find the answer only when we live in a manner appropriate to human nature: by Reason.

John wants to focus his mind and efforts on the best and highest occupation of his soul. That is "the Self." The individual's life and being is the highest occupation of his soul; and that, by his very nature.

Attack on Altruism

My mom is an Objectivist and the other voice of rationality in my developing philosophy. She also rails on Christianity for its Altruism. Very few in our culture identify Altruism as a vice, but Rand does. John explained her definitions to me. She pulls no punches in expressing what she dislikes about it.

> *Altruism declares that any action taken for the benefit of others is good, and any action taken for one's own benefit is evil. Thus the beneficiary of an action is the only criterion of moral value—and so long as that beneficiary is anybody other than oneself, anything goes.*[3]

Rand's villains constantly cloak their manipulative, unreasonable, slovenly, self-gratifying motives in sappy, highbrow, moralistic rhetoric. The villain you love to hate is James Taggart, Dagny's brother and the head of Taggart Transcontinental. The philosophy he throws in Dagny's face is Altruism. He responds to her passion for making money by saying, "Selfish greed for profit is a thing of the past. It has been generally conceded that the interests of society as a whole must always be placed first in any business undertaking..."[4]

In characteristic hypocritical form, he condescends to marry Cherryl, a diner waitress. He wants to appear selfless, and altruistically "rise above" modern class categories. He marries her to make himself feel like the man he knows he is not. However, not only are his aspirations contrary to human nature and dishonest, he fails to achieve them. He ends up feeling even worse about himself and never gets the public accolades he craves. James is what Ayn Rand calls a second-hander. He refuses to live from the joy that comes through achieving what he values for its own sake. Instead, he lives secondhand from the assessment and approval of others.

Specifically, Ayn Rand rejects Altruism as a principle of *self*-sacrifice, a principle that says "…man has no right to exist for his own sake, that service to others is the only justification of his existence, and that self-sacrifice is his highest moral duty, virtue, and value."[5] In *Unrugged Individualism*, David Kelley uses Jesus as the example of the quintessential Altruist.

> *[T]he paradigm of altruism is complete self-immolation, as in the story of Jesus, who died to atone for the sins of mankind, or the martyrdom of the Christian saints; or the demands of totalitarian leaders in this century that their citizens sacrifice their freedom, prosperity, and even their lives for the good of the nation.*[6]

Kelley's words illustrate a profound, but not uncommon, misunderstanding of Christianity that Rand herself concurs with wholeheartedly.

> *There is a great, basic contradiction in the teachings of Jesus. Jesus was one of the first great teachers to proclaim the basic principle of individualism—the inviolate sanctity of man's soul, and the salvation of one's soul as one's first concern and highest goal; this means—one's ego and the integrity of one's ego. But when it came to the next question, a code of ethics to observe for the salvation of one's soul—(this means: what must one do in actual practice in order to save one's soul?)—Jesus (or perhaps His interpreters) gave men a code of altruism, that is, a code which told them that in order to save one's soul, one must love or help or live for others.*[7]

Where Rand is utterly correct is in her recognition that Jesus affirmed the unique "sanctity of man's soul." But I also knew where she misinterpreted the message of the Gospel. I couldn't leave this discrepancy unaddressed.

"But John, the Gospel doesn't present right and wrong the way Ayn Rand says it does." That made John pause. It was something Dad argued so many times, times when I had always taken the other side. Now it was my own perspective, and it made sense. I said, "Ayn Rand equates the Gospel to Altruism, which it simply isn't."

John got right to the point. "You mean to tell me that Jesus didn't say 'Love your neighbor'?"

"Oh, He did," I said. "But that's only the second part of it."

"If you mean 'love yourself first, and then love your neighbor' then we're almost on the same page here," John said. "What *do* you mean?"

"Altruism says that you measure right and wrong by who benefits: something is right if it benefits others, and wrong if it benefits me. That's Altruism, not Christianity."

"Oh, come on. What's the difference?" John asked, unintentionally sounding dismissive.

"There is a big difference!" I said, surprised at my own defensiveness. "It's that God is at the center, not other people. According to Rand's script, the individual is the lead in his own life's play." John nodded. I continued, "In Altruism, Others are the lead in the play that is his life; he is a bystander. And in the production of the Christian's life play, Jesus is the lead." While John may not have agreed with that, he certainly understood it.

God, the Egoist

> *An egoist... lives for himself. In this, I can agree with the worst of Christian moralists. The questions are only: 1) what constitutes living for oneself? and 2) if the first is answered my way, i.e., living for one's highest values, then isn't living for oneself the highest type of living, the only real living and the only ethical living possible?*[8]
>
> — Ayn Rand

I have always been intrigued by Rand's arguments for "rational self-interest." When I first encountered the Christian message, I assumed that it was the antithesis of Rand's philosophy in every way. I had read the New and Old Testaments, but not from a strictly Randian perspective. Asking questions about the character of God in a way that would honor the Randian thought process became a challenge and an adventure.

At first, the idea of God as a selfish being, in the Randian sense, contradicted my understanding of Christianity. But the Scriptures bore out this understanding. God is *for* Himself, and He makes no bones about it. He wields everything He created for His pleasure, His own benefit.

> *In framing your questions, please try to observe whether they are based on and imply some premise improperly accepted as an axiom. Or, in other words, please check your premises.*[9]
>
> —*Ayn Rand*

The Psalmist writes, "Our God is in heaven; He does whatever pleases Him."[10] In the writing of the prophet Isaiah, the LORD says, "For my own sake, for my own sake, I do this. How can I let myself be defamed? I will not yield my glory to another."[11] Over and over, I see God doing whatever acknowledges His value above all things, and makes it known. Again, the LORD says, "Bring my sons from afar and my daughters from the ends of the earth—everyone who is called by my name, whom I created for my glory, whom I formed and made."[12] All that is true, noble, right, pure, lovely, admirable, and praiseworthy brings Joy to the God of the Bible.

> *"I am the LORD, who exercises kindness, justice and righteousness on earth, for in these I delight," declares the LORD.*
> — Jeremiah 9:24 (NIV)

In the best possible definition of the term, God is selfish. John Piper expounds on this readily misunderstood notion:

> *To say his glory is uppermost in his own affections means that he puts a greater value on it than on anything else. He delights in his glory above all things.*[13]

God puts Himself first. Every aspect of God's character is supreme in its quality and value. As the most supremely valuable being, He would deny Reality, embracing falsehood, if He did not take infinite delight in the worth of His own glory. It's right to take delight in a person in proportion to the excellence of that person's glory.

Nevertheless, in my discussions with Christians, the term Selfishness seldom connotes something positive. But God's character, as described in the Bible, made a connection for me: Selfishness, in the Randian sense of rational self-interest, is foundational to Gospel Christianity. Whether a Christian could recite John Galt's oath, however, was unclear to me.[14] I still had questions.

Self-Denial

Dad was not entirely sold on the Randian idea of Selfishness applying to the Gospel. He showed me several places where Jesus calls for self-denial. "I'm struggling," I admitted. "The Bible clearly displays compelling reasons to pursue our own self-interest in a relationship with God. There is a lot of evidence for that. But Jesus himself calls for self-denial. I don't see that as compatible with my interests."

Jesus said,

> *If anyone would come after me, let him deny himself and take up his cross and follow me. For whoever would save his life will lose it, but whoever loses his life for my sake and the gospel's will save it.*[15]

> — Mark 8:34-35 (NIV)

For years, I labored with the tension between denying myself and pursuing Joy. It seemed to me not only an internal inconsistency within Christianity, but also an insurmountable barrier to reconciling the world views of Dad and John. Not surprisingly, Dad's exhortation came with passion: "Look to Jesus." And John's advice seemed to channel Rand: "Check your premises." They came from different perspectives, yet something compelled me to apply the fatherly advice of each one.

Looking to Jesus, I continued to give consideration to the Gospels. There is a scene where Jesus teaches about the impossibility of achieving kingdom status through human effort. The Apostle Peter, a future pillar of the Church, appeals to the teaching of Jesus on self-denial when he responded to Jesus this way:

"We have left everything and followed you."
— Mark 10:28 (MSG)

Checking my premises, I examined Jesus's attitude to Peter's obviously "sacrificial" attitude. It struck me that Jesus didn't praise and validate Peter, but rebuked him. Jesus said, "No one who sacrifices house, brothers, sisters, mother, father, children, land," for the sake of Him and the Gospel, will regret it. "They'll get it all back, but multiplied many times."[16] Why did Jesus rebuke Peter for thinking in terms of sacrifice? Hadn't Jesus Himself demanded "self-denial?"

Not that Ayn Rand is the pinnacle of Christian thinking, but what would Peter have said had he been rationally self-interested? The response of Jesus indicates that the way to think about self-denial is to deny yourself only a lesser good for a greater good. And so it is that Jesus's definition of Sacrifice rules out all self-pity. This is in fact just what the texts on self-denial teach.

Listen carefully: Unless a grain of wheat is buried in the ground, dead to the world, it is never any more than a grain of

139

wheat. But if it is buried, it sprouts and reproduces itself many times over. In the same way, anyone who holds on to life just as it is destroys that life. But if you let it go, reckless in your love, you'll have it forever, real and eternal.

— John 12:24-25 (MSG)

Saint Augustine captured the paradox in these words: If you love your soul, there is danger of its being destroyed. Do not love it, since you do not want it to be destroyed. In not wanting it to be destroyed you love it.[17]

This paradox was the basis for Jesus's argument. He does not ask us to be indifferent to whether we are destroyed. On the contrary, He assumes that the very longing for true life[18] will move us to deny ourselves all the lesser pleasures and comforts of life. If we were indifferent to the value of God's gift of life, we would dishonor it. The measure of your longing for life is the amount of comfort you are willing to give up to enjoy God's presence: the gift of *real life*. That is the God-centered value of self-denial.

Sacrifice is a Randian Vice

When I encountered her notoriously titled book of essays, *The Virtue of Selfishness*, I was put off, but only slightly. Because of John's kitchen table discourses, which I lamented at the time, I knew the ramifications of Ayn Rand's rational self-interest. My friends were repulsed that I thought Selfishness was good. They were not at all curious about the intellectual exercise; but they were riveted by the novelty, like it was a freakish abnormality. You would have thought I said, "Oh, the other day I decided to start growing a tail. It's up to 16 inches, now." They refused to take me seriously, until I explained. Perhaps my friends felt the same oddness that I felt when Dad talked about Jesus so intimately: a novelty that was somehow attracting and repelling at once. Ayn Rand's perspective on Sacrifice, as well as John and Mom's, was quite apart from Dad's. Once again, I was torn.

Since virtue, to you, consists of sacrifice... you have sacrificed all those evils which you held as the cause of your plight. You have sacrificed justice to mercy. You have sacrificed independence to unity. You have sacrificed reason to faith. You have sacrificed wealth to need. You have sacrificed self-esteem to self-denial. You have sacrificed happiness to duty.[19]

The passage from John Galt's speech spells out the consequences of bad philosophy, as does the notorious description of the Twentieth Century Motor Company, discussed in the fifth chapter, "Capitalism." It also illustrates Rand's misdiagnosis of Sacrifice. For her, self-denial could only be equated with Sacrifice.

"Sacrifice" is the surrender of a greater value for the sake of a lesser one or of a nonvalue. Thus, altruism gauges a man's virtue by the degree to which he surrenders, renounces or betrays his values (since help to a stranger or an enemy is regarded as more virtuous, less "selfish," than help to those one loves). The rational principle of conduct is the exact opposite: always act in accordance with the hierarchy of your values, and never sacrifice a greater value to a lesser one.[20]

Because Ayn Rand sees the self as the individual's highest occupation, the best thing that an individual can do is occupy his mind, will, and emotions with his own personal happiness. To do this, he needs to know what will make him the happiest. Is there ever any room for Sacrifice in the Objectivist mindset, in the pursuit of what makes someone happy? Not in the way Rand defines it. By her definition, Sacrifice seems wholly indefensible. As a matter of fact, she calls it a *vice.*

A friend of mine worked with a senior executive named Bill, who was an outstanding mentor. He was successful and highly knowledgeable as well as consummately competent. He had a reputation for seeking out ways to enhance others' strengths, deferring to them and supporting them graciously—even in business situations where he could easily have commanded the limelight. Bill exemplified my friend's definition of Sacrifice in the corporate environment and he even testified to those very characteristics at Bill's funeral.

If John were evaluating Bill's example of Sacrifice according to Rand's definition, he would conclude that Bill undervalued his own success. Rand would say that, whether or not he knew it, Bill allowed the Altruistic world view to drag him into the misplaced ethics of Sacrifice. He subordinated his own life to the incompetence of others who lacked the technical skill and ability to achieve success without the misplaced favor of a smarter, more capable individual. As it turned out, Rand was right about Bill. He could have acquired more financial wealth, been recognized more for his talents and contributions to the company, and been a more prominent player. By foregoing these good things, he set aside the resources that could have contributed to a more fulfilling life. His life, in Rand's estimation, should be paramount. Instead, he subjected a greater value, his own achievement and happiness, to a lesser value, the well-being of another.

Most of us, however, think about Sacrifice differently than this. Certainly, it involves surrendering one thing for the benefit of another, but it invariably involves gaining something more valuable. The noun form of the word "sacrifice" refers to the thing lost. Take a concrete example from baseball. A "sacrifice" is a bunt that allows a runner to advance one base while the batter is put out. The batter surrenders his "getting on base" to something that he and the team value more highly. He's not giving up something that he values more highly than what he's getting. He's trading up! On this point, Rand's definition is at odds with the rest of the world. From the opposite vantage point, it would be selfish (maybe even foolish) for the batter to assume that getting on base was more valuable than the lead-runner scoring.

"Selfishness" equates to self-interested. As Ayn Rand uses the word, even Christians are "selfish." But because Rand's definition of Sacrifice is more narrow than the common usage of the idea, the more common understanding of Sacrifice makes it easier to order our values. Most would agree that we should never subjugate something of greater value to something of lesser value. It's a "no brainer," a straw man. It's obviously bad. John's Objectivist repulsion for sacrificing a greater to a lesser good is actually right on and surprisingly consistent with Dad's Christianity. Dad values service, but the idea that all service is Sacrifice is entirely unthinking and illogical. On the other hand, intentionally doing without one thing in order to gain something else of greater value is clearly virtuous by both the Christian and the Randian definition.

Religion versus the Gospel

Sacrifice, as it's practiced in what I would call "legalistic religion," means saying, "I'm going to give up the bad things, do the good things, and get what I want from God." For example, I will live a morally pure life, stop sleeping around, read the Bible and go to church, and then God will give me a good life. Things will go well for me. Under this version, I'm making a sacrifice, but it's to get something greater than what I give up. A slightly different version says that, if I do all these things, nothing bad will happen to me. The latter might be fear-based while the former may not, but what's similar is the end: it's all about getting the life I want. There's a veneer of Godward-ness, but it's not really about God at all. While Rand seems to equate Christian Sacrifice with this "religious" twist in the path, the true Gospel points to something altogether different. David Livingstone said this:

People talk of the sacrifice I have made in spending much of my life in Africa. Is that a sacrifice which brings its own blest

*reward in healthful activity, the consciousness of doing good, peace of mind, and a bright hope of a glorious destiny hereafter?...
I have never made a sacrifice![21]*

Here, Livingstone is asserting that what Christians do is not sacrifice at all! If Christians follow Rand's definition of Sacrifice, they would abandon the practice altogether and wipe the word "sacrifice" from their vocabulary. Eugene Peterson:

The Bible begins with God speaking creation and us into being. It continues with God entering into personalized and complex relationships with us, helping and blessing us, teaching and training us, correcting and disciplining us, loving and saving us. This is not an escape from reality but a plunge into more reality—a sacrificial but altogether better life all the way.[22]

So, I understood Rand's view that Sacrifice is bad. Whenever an individual places anything or anyone else's interest above his own, in order to further that other person's interest above that of the individual, he commits a great vice, known as Sacrifice. It's not that the Objectivist refuses to do something to benefit someone else. However, doing something to benefit someone else exclusively—with no benefit accruing to oneself—is wasted effort. Even worse, doing anything to benefit another, *at the expense of* oneself is a vice.

As Rand characterizes Sacrifice, it is a part of altruistic philosophy, the morality of death, and indicative of gloom and doom. Rand uses this definition consistently throughout her fiction and nonfiction. Nevertheless, it doesn't describe Jesus's sacrifice, and consequently, does not do justice to the Christian definition.

We call it Sacrifice when we give up something to gain something else of greater value. But the object of the Sacrifice—what we gain—is always greater than what we give up. Or at least, we perceive it to be so. In fact, it's always possible to trace our Sacrifice back to a selfish motive. There are at least two ways that Objectivists criticize Christians; one is based in fact, and one in misunderstanding.

Duty versus Pleasure

Two of the reasons that Rand objects to Christianity are Sacrifice and Duty. In her mind, they go hand in hand.

"She has a point," I said to John, "but only to the extent that you buy her definition of Sacrifice. And that's an odd one, in my opinion." I read from one of her essays. "It's like she creates a straw man and uses it to condemn sacrifice."

> *"Sacrifice" is the surrender of a greater value for the sake of a lesser one or of a nonvalue.[23]*

"Why would anyone subject a greater value to a lesser one?" I asked John. "That's just it," he said. "They wouldn't knowingly do it."

Pursuing, I asked, "Knowingly? How could someone miss something so obvious?"

He answered in a matter-of-fact tone, "I think it all comes back to philosophy. To the extent that an altruistic view of the world influences your thinking, you're going to overvalue others relative to yourself, or undervalue yourself relative to others. In my evaluation, that's a mistake."

I could see his point. As I remembered the life of Sacrifice I had seen in people like Bill and Dad, I wondered what would account for it. Ignorance? Was Dad undervaluing himself, lacking in self-esteem? Not likely. Delusions of inferiority were not part of Dad's thinking. For that matter, Dad didn't exude an air of superiority either.

John had one word to answer my question. One word characterized the motivations of those who sacrifice: Duty. Ayn Rand blames Immanuel Kant.

The arch-advocate of "duty" is Immanuel Kant; he went so much farther than other theorists that they seem innocently benevolent by comparison. "Duty," he holds, is the only standard of virtue; but virtue is not its own reward: if a reward is involved, it is no longer virtue. The only moral motivation, he holds, is devotion to duty for duty's sake... without any concern for "inclination" [desire] or self-interest.[24]

Rand goes after Kant's idea of Duty as "one of the most destructive anti-concepts in the history of moral philosophy." It destroys Reason because it is "the moral necessity to perform certain actions" based on "obedience to some higher authority, without regard to any personal goal, motive, desire or interest."[25] What's more, she equates Christianity with the religion of Immanuel Kant.

Even though Kant secularizes the concept of Duty, Rand believes that "the authority of God's will has been ascribed to earthly entities, such as parents, country, State, mankind, etc., their alleged supremacy still rests on nothing but a mystic edict."[26] Some argue that the Kantian perspective paints Christians as subordinating their own needs to the needs of others in order to secure rewards in heaven; but for Rand this would be a "nonvalue," because heaven doesn't exist.

As a Christian, Dad disagreed with Rand's assessment of heaven, but also rejected the Kantian perspective of Duty, saying "Duty is not Christianity's highest call." It may have been Dad who shared with me a section of a sermon by C. S. Lewis entitled, "The Weight of Glory."

If there lurks in most modern minds the notion that to desire our own good and earnestly to hope for the enjoyment of it is a bad thing, I submit that this notion has crept in from Kant and the Stoics and is no part of the Christian faith. Indeed, if we consider the unblushing promises of reward and the staggering nature of

*the rewards promised in the Gospels, it would seem that Our Lord
finds our desires not too strong, but too weak.*[27]

The distinction is between those whose motivation to follow Jesus is
between their Duty to Him as their Savior and Lord, and those who follow
Him because doing so is their greatest pleasure. Just as distinguished above
with Sacrifice, Dad makes a distinction between "Religion" and the Gospel
in the realm of Duty.

Religion

Rand's concept of Duty entails an obligation to do something contrary to my
nature: as an act of my will, to grit my teeth and do something under duress,
out of guilt, or not strictly what I would choose if I were truly free. Religion
can be summed up, "I do, and then God owes me." The order is crucial. First,
I perform according to some right standard and establish a record based on my
achievement of the standard. The standard could be anything: the Law of God
or the teachings of Jesus. Or, it could be someone's life example, a hero or an
ideology, even a philosophy. It could even be, as Francis Shaffer articulated, the
cumulative "shoulds" and "oughts" I have perpetrated on others. They provide
a standard of their own. The point is that I keep my end of the implied contract by living up to the standard, and then God or Fate or Fortune or whatever,
confers some deserved blessing because I've earned it. This is, by far, the most
widely practiced definition of Religion in the world today. Consequently, the
most prolific use of Sacrifice and Duty figures into its practice. Rand does not
distinguish, as Dad does, between Religion and Christianity.

The Gospel Reverses the Order

The Gospel turns the order around. Instead of making my performance
against the standard the determining factor of my life's value, the Gospel

says that Jesus has met the standard in my place and exchanged His perfect record for my imperfect one. God doesn't evaluate me based on what I sacrificed to achieve an acceptable, or even perfect, standard. He takes the initiative. He meets the standard as my substitute. My position is established, apart from anything I do or achieve. The Gospel message says God does this for anyone who looks to Jesus to play out that truth in his or her life.

The Difference

"So, how does Duty play out differently in the life of the person under the Gospel?" I asked Dad.

"The key relates to ends and means," he said. "The religious person sees God as the means to another end; for example, so nothing bad happens in my life. If I perform according to the standard, then I will avoid suffering, or anything *really* bad." That sounded like Christianity to me, or at least the version I had observed growing up, but he went on to say that the Gospel portrays God as the end toward which everything else is a means.

> *Our pleasure and our duty*
> *Though opposite before,*
> *Since we have seen His beauty,*
> *Are joined to part no more.*
> *It is our highest pleasure,*
> *No less than duty's call,*
> *To love Him beyond measure,*
> *And serve Him with our all.*[28]
> *To see the law by Christ fulfilled*
> *And hear His pardoning voice,*
> *Transforms a slave into a child*
> *And duty into choice.*[29]

—William Cowper

Tim Keller gives a great example of this when he talks about his relationship to Mozart over the years.

You're glorifying something when you find it beautiful for what it is in itself. Its beauty compels you to adore it, to have your imagination captured by it. This happened to me with Mozart. I listened to Mozart to get an A in music appreciation in college. I had to get good grades to get a good job, so in other words, I listened to Mozart to make money. But today I am quite willing to spend money just to listen to Mozart, not because it's useful to me anymore but because it's beautiful in itself. It's no longer a means to an end.[30]

When anything is an ultimate end, the thing that makes us able to receive all other elements of life with gratefulness and contentment, we find ourselves making everything else in our lives serve that end. It doesn't seem like a Duty because it all points to something that we value much more.

Dad tried to explain the difference for a long time. In the past, I didn't understand the distinction. I thought that the Gospel was primarily about moral reformation: living a good life, pleasing God out of a sense of duty. I don't want to minimize that motivation; God is worthy of our devotion. While a life with Jesus is not less than pleasing Him, it's much, much more.

If the rules or the standards we set become the primary focus, there are really only two alternatives that can result. Both of these bring a kind of "curse": depending on whether we live up to the standard or whether we fall short. If we live up to the standard, we elevate ourselves. Confidence is good, but not if it leads to arrogance and the renunciation of others who "have less value" because they don't live up to "the standard that I have achieved." Taken to its extreme, that attitude throws life out of perspective. It brings a curse on itself, not the least of which is alienation and isolation.

If we don't live up to the standard, we put ourselves down and harbor "low self-esteem." If we cannot perform—and value is based on performance—we conclude that we have no value. Some consider that to be "humility," but it's really just self-deprecation. We may avoid the "curse" of arrogance and self-aggrandizement that leads to alienation, but we do not see ourselves as Jesus sees us. Both curses are self-defeating.

The Gospel understands both the curse of arrogance and the curse of self-deprecation. Both separate us from ourselves and each other. Under the curse, we cannot have the intimacy for which we were created. The good news is that God deals with the curse. The religious person who follows rules to gain favor with God focuses his life on himself as an end: what *he* does, what *he* earns. The secular version of this person is the Objectivist. Though everyone wants to focus mind, will, and emotions on the highest possible occupation, the noticeable and irreconcilable difference is that we disagree on what that is. As the soul's highest value, the Objectivist sees the life of the individual; the Christian sees God Himself. One is relational; the other is not.

The principle runs through all life from top to bottom. Give up your self, and you will find your real self. Lose your life and you will save it. Submit to death, death of your ambitions and favourite wishes every day and death of your whole body in the end: submit with every fibre of your being, and you will find eternal life. Keep back nothing. Nothing that you have not given away will ever be really yours. Nothing in you that has not died will ever be raised from the dead. Look for yourself, and you will find in the long run only hatred, loneliness, despair, rage, ruin, and decay. But look for Christ and you will find Him, and with Him everything else thrown in.[31]

— C. S. Lewis

Worship

It follows naturally, and even logically, from this understanding of relationship to the Almighty that the response to God is worship. As John Piper points out in his classic, *Desiring God*, God continually commands humans to pursue the highest possible occupation of our souls. The reason for the exhortation relates to our nature, how we are wired. It seemed so Randian to pursue the highest occupation of my mind, will, and emotions, even if Rand did not agree that our nature stems from the way God created us (although she did agree that all humans *have* a nature). The Old and New Testaments continually speak about God as that Highest Occupation: "Delight yourself in the Lord." As a consequence, sacrificing our time and energy to praise God is, for a Christian, surrendering something precious to gain something even more precious. At this very juncture lies the fork in the path.

> *This—thought Dagny, with a sickened amusement—was the spectacle of the sincerity of the dishonest. The most fraudulent part of the fraud was that they meant it. They were offering Galt the best that their view of existence could offer, they were trying to tempt him with that which was their dream of life's highest fulfillment: this spread of mindless adulation, the unreality of this enormous pretense—approval without standards, tribute without content, honor without causes, admiration without reasons, love without a code of values.*[32]
>
> *Delight yourself in the* Lord *and he will give you the desires of your heart.*
>
> — Psalm 37:4 (NIV)

Dad's understanding of Christian worship involves Sacrifice, praise, and something else that took me two decades to understand. Worship, from the Latin, connotes the idea of "shaping one's worth." Everyone's worth is shaped by something. Rand's villains tried to tempt her über-hero with what they thought would and should shape his worth. John Galt, however, did not for a moment consider their unreality. He assessed his value—his worth as an individual—based on his own mind and his capacity to produce and sustain his life. When I looked at Dad's life, I saw that he valued his productive capacity and independence enormously, but ultimately discovered their limited ability to sustain the human soul.

I had become so engrossed in some aspects of Ayn Rand's philosophy; I realized that I let the idea of my ability to achieve, produce, and "get things done" shape my worth. It defined my value as a person. Dad pointed out several good things in his life that he had let shape him. None of those were God. His journey, and subsequently mine, entailed dismantling these "idols" and embracing God's value-shaping activity in the context of a new relationship.

Ayn Rand, when speaking of Dominique Francon and Howard Roark in *The Fountainhead*, writes, "her love for him is essentially worship, it becomes her religion, it becomes her reconciliation with life, with humanity and with herself—but not until many years later."[33]

Disdain for worship is behind many objections to Christian practice. Rand saw the Christian as piously expressing hollow sentiment or ritualistic mysticism, and this kind of dutiful, robotic behavior disgusted her.

> *Since man must establish his own values, accepting a value above himself makes him low and worthless. Allow nothing to stand between you and the world. The worship of something above you (like God) is an escape, a switch of responsibility—to permit you anything.*[34]

Perhaps Rand considered the high ritual of the Roman Catholic or Anglican Church, or the pietistic, monastic rituals of the fifteenth-century monks when she made the comments above. Traditionally viewed as the poetry, if not the manual for the worship of God's people, the Psalms are unanimously part of the praise and worship of Judeo-Christian worshippers throughout history. Notwithstanding Rand's comments, Dad believes that recognizing and praising God's supreme value is what completes the highest experience of satisfaction.

> *I thought of [praise] in terms of compliment, approval, or the giving of honor. I had never noticed that all enjoyment spontaneously overflows into praise... The world rings with praise—lovers praising their mistresses, readers their favorite poet, walkers praising the countryside, players praising their favorite game...*
>
> *I think we delight to praise what we enjoy because the praise not merely expresses but completes the enjoyment; it is its appointed consummation.[35]*

John Piper augments Lewis's expression by stating his own Christian convictions. He says,

> *Praising God, the highest calling of humanity and our eternal vocation, did not involve the renunciation but rather the consummation of the joy I so desired [before and after my conversion]. We have a name for those who try to praise when they have no pleasure in the object. We call them hypocrites. This fact—that praise means consummate pleasure and that the highest end of man is to drink deeply of this pleasure—was perhaps the most liberating discovery I ever made.[36]*

Conclusion

Rand's use of the word "Selfishness" may be eye-catching and provocative. It may have engaged the critics. But it's not the best word for what Rand advocates in her writing. She advocates self-interest; and that's a word that doesn't draw a lot of condemnation these days. It's taken for granted that people act to benefit themselves. I will act in a manner that will benefit myself, in a manner that is according to my nature as a human being. But again, what do those actions entail? The answer is different for each world view, but the motivation is the same: What will benefit me the most? The answer is to act in line with my nature. What is "acting in line with my nature?" The Christian says, with Augustine, "Our hearts are restless until they find their rest in Thee, O Lord."[37] The Objectivist says, "I will not be truly satisfied until I esteem myself higher than anything else."

My soul's state of "Oneness" with God

To follow the Randian philosophy, I must choose the highest value and give myself wholly to it. If, as Rand says, I am my own highest value, and my soul is the most valuable part of me, it will maximize the value (to me) of my soul by putting it in the most valuable state possible, the state of "salvation" or "oneness with God."

Or, on the contrary, God doesn't exist and neither does my soul, so nothing I think, say, or do matters at all, given that I and everything I've ever been will cease to exist upon my physical death. The conclusion to that declaration, it seems to me, is that I should just go crawl into a hole somewhere and wait to die. Or sell my house, blow all the cash on a weekend in Vegas and then kill myself. Or whatever. I find it hard to see what matters since I wouldn't remember any of it anyway. A good Objectivist, my stepfather, perhaps, might implore me with "You should seek the highest values in life in order to maximize the value of your time in the world." But I just can't buy that anymore, because if it's all over when I die then that "value" dies with me. My kids are doomed to the same fate, so leaving "stuff" for them is pointless, since they're just gonna' die too... and the same goes for everybody else's kids, ad infinatum.

I tend toward choosing Door #1.

9

JOY

*Happiness is possible only to a rational man, the man
who desires nothing but rational goals, seeks nothing but
rational values and finds his joy in nothing but rational
actions.*[1]

— John Galt

How amazing is it that I have become a Christian? The unlikelihood
that a controlling misfit, self-absorbed and always-needing-to-be-right,
could experience the freedom to admit and even embrace my brokenness!
It amazes me when I think about it! Release, relief, rest… finally. "He who
knew no sin, but became sin for us."[2]

Vulnerability. For the first time, I see that I need it. Weak? Yes, but
I want the courage to come to terms with my guilt and my shame. For the

first time, I can face my past failures as well as my present character flaws that seem so intolerable I must deny them, ignore them, and not deal with them authentically. Then I remember that God created me in His perfect image. There is wholeness and completeness in my future. But I do not move there until I face the emptiness, the lack of Meaning. When I see my emptiness and truly understand, when I feel the emotional weight of what I lack, only then can I appreciate and enter into the longing. The only wholeness and fullness that can overcome the dark cave inside me is that which comes from knowing God.

To know God is to know and experience who I was created to be and what I was designed to do. There is Joy in that kind of freedom, in finding my completion; and it's much more than happiness. Aristotle talked about this. It's the complete realization of what I am intrinsically designed to be: my purpose. It's realizing my highest purpose and potential, and there is no higher pursuit. God doesn't say, "I know that you already have a full and meaningful and joyful life, but I want you to give that up in order to fulfill your duty to Me." Not even remotely close. He says, "You will experience the Joy that I have designed you to experience—your highest pursuit—when you pursue Me." God has made us experience the fullest, highest soul meaning and purpose in Him. I remind myself of this truth every day.

Delight yourself in the LORD, and He will give you the desires of your heart.

— Psalm 37:4, (NIV)

I think God promises that we will receive our highest delight and fulfillment when we delight in Him because He *is* that delight.

Neither does God say, "Do your duty, live worthy and righteous, and then I will grant you a fulfilling life." I tend to want to see it that way, because that puts me in control. I imagine that I control the outcome. With that mindset, I do what I need to do (myself) and then God owes me. I liked the idea of God being in debt to me. But, again, that is not based on Reality.

And while it's a lot more comfortable to be in control and it's tempting to embrace the illusion, Ayn Rand herself taught me that "wishing won't make it so."[3]

So I am left with Reality: relentless, boldfaced, and sometimes harsh. My hope, however, is not in some impersonal idea or concept of what is real. Instead, I am overcome and overwhelmed with the generosity and compassion and symmetry and beauty of the Immortal God of the Universe, who has condescended to communicate to the finite, fallible creation, to discover my complete fulfillment and uncontainable Joy in Him.

I was created for Joy. I'm wired for it. We all are. Ayn Rand sensed this, even though she used a different vocabulary. She wrote explicitly about Joy in her fiction and her nonfiction, but she often used the word "happiness" to mean what Aristotle meant by the same Greek word translated "joy" in the Bible. Whichever term she utilized, I would emphasize that Rand *approaches* the idea of Joy, but, like a mathematical limit, never arrives at it.

Happiness…versus Joy

"Happiness" seems attainable for most people, but it's also fickle, shallow, and fleeting. As the word implies, happiness is associated with happenings, happenstance, luck, and fortune. If circumstances are favorable, you are happy; if not, you're unhappy. Joy is something altogether different and permanent. Dad knew this. "My soul's satisfaction doesn't depend on circumstances. It's a good thing, too." I knew where he was going. "If it depended on 'good fortune,' I would never be happy." Maybe "never" was an exaggeration, but his load of hardship was incomprehensible to me. He had a point.

Then Dad said, "My joy won't be shaken."

"But really," I said, "how can you say that?" We always got into it sooner or later. "Why do you make those categorical statements? It just sounds so arrogant and narrow." It was one thing to say "I try to be steady and bal-anced." He was that. But he was saying that he would continue to be, no matter what.

It was a recurring theme. I got the sense that both fathers were utterly entrenched in their convictions about happiness— and every other topic we talked about. Where was the openness to others? I could have stomached it, if it were not so blatant. How about a little humility to counterbalance the arrogance once in a while? I had seen their shortcomings. Neither father claimed perfection, but neither seemed to own his brokenness, either. It took a while, but over time, with Dad at least, I saw a consistent underlying theme of humility. At first, I thought it was false humility, like he was really just kidding himself and trying to pretend that he was "unworthy," some Christian thing about not puffing himself up. One day, though, I under-stood it.

The confidence that I interpreted as arrogance came from a deep sense of validation from the most important person in his life: Jesus. The humility that I considered a charade was not fake at all. He understood that his ability, achievement, validation—in short, his Joy!—did not originate with him, but were a gift from one far greater than himself. And in that relation-ship, Dad was being changed from the inside out. His very perception of "self" was being transformed.

Joy is different from pleasure, or even happiness. Joy is not fleeting, like pleasure, or dependent on circumstances, like happiness. The latter depends on the experience of the moment, or even reflecting about a moment past. Joy stays with you and becomes part of you, and in so being, Joy is inextri-cably tied to Meaning, no less so for Rand than for the Christian. While it will be necessary to clarify her terminology, whatever Rand's understanding of Joy, it was her highest pursuit. She looked for it in ideas, intellect, phi-losophy, engaging in a cause, and even in sex.

God of Pleasure or Pleasure as God?

Pleasure and mere happiness are what Tim Keller considers penultimate "goods." If we imagine that they can sustain our souls, if we imbue ultimate status upon the penultimate, all of the good we see around us can drive us to despair. Even the title of his book, *Counterfeit Gods*, provokes thought on these matters. What is true, and what is counterfeit? What merely mimics or mocks the genuine? What qualifies as a god? The essence of Keller's message is that Money, Sex, Power… can each be a source of great pleasure and bring a measure of happiness to ourselves and others, but none of those provides deep, abiding Joy that transcends human circumstance.

Joy is not fleeting. In asserting this, both world views rise above the philosophy of mere hedonism. The good is not "whatever gives you pleasure." Neither world view makes a god out of pleasure, because pleasure is not a first cause, only a consequence. John Piper gets it right when he follows God's idea of happiness.

> *The pleasure [the Christian Hedonist seeks] is the pleasure that is in God Himself. He is the end of our search, not the means to some further end. Our exceeding joy is He, the Lord—not the streets of gold or the reunion with relatives or any blessing of heaven. Christian Hedonism does not reduce God to a key that unlocks a treasure chest of gold and silver. Rather, it seeks to transform the heart so that "the Almighty will be your gold and your precious silver."[4]*

People use the expression "genuine happiness," to mean a state that transcends circumstantial happiness. This meaning of happiness is at the center of everyone's deepest longings. Because Rand uses the terms happiness and joy more or less in reverse of my understanding, it can be somewhat confusing, yet both Objectivism and Gospel Christianity tell us that true happiness is an essential virtue. Both agree with Pascal's universal statement

to that effect. The satisfaction of the Objectivist proceeds from his achievement, while the Christian's Joy proceeds from God. In the following passage,
Rand defines happiness as "the successful state of life"[5] in which the experience of joy can be found.

> *Happiness is that state of consciousness which proceeds from
> the achievement of one's values... Happiness is possible only to
> a rational man, the man who desires nothing but rational goals,
> seeks nothing but rational values and finds his joy in nothing but
> rational actions.[6]*
>
> — John Galt

While even a casual observer can't miss the Objectivist's unmistakable quest for personal happiness, it comes up short of the quest
that true Gospel Christianity has at its heart. Put in the context
of the Biblical narrative (what God is doing in the world from Creation
through Redemption), the Bible is replete with souls pursuing nothing short
of unbridled ecstasy using God's very own prescription. As Blaise Pascal
wrote, this is inevitable in any honest world view.

> *All men seek happiness [Joy]. This is without exception.
> Whatever different means they employ, they all tend to this end.
> The cause of some going to war, and of others avoiding it, is the
> same desire in both, attended with different views. The will never
> takes the least step but to this object. This is the motive of every
> action of every man, even of those who hang themselves.[7]*

Non-contradictory Joy

One of the reasons that Ayn Rand's fictional characters seem somewhat
unreal or flat is that they purport to be experiencing Joy (what she calls

happiness), but it's just not there. They remind me of someone who genuinely senses that he should appreciate something, but doesn't; like my fourteen-year-old nephew, for instance, acting really excited to get clothes on his birthday. In her journal, writing with the most passionate of language, Rand characterizes John Galt by the joy he experiences from his achievements. His level of exuberance seems to be rooted in something that does not actually warrant exuberance.

> *Joy in living—the peculiar, deeply natural, serene, all-pervading joy in living which he alone possesses so completely in the story (the other strikers have it in lesser degree, almost as reflections of that which, in him, is the source). His joy is all-pervading in the sense that it underlies all his actions and emotions, it is an intrinsic, inseparable part of his nature (like the color of his hair or eyes). It is present even when he suffers (particularly in the torture scene)—that is when the nature and quality of his joy in living is startling and obvious, it is not resignation or acceptance of suffering, but a denial of it, a triumph over it.[8]*

In the abstract, Rand's ideas are good, since she truly longs for Joy. But she doesn't pull it off in her writing, because she wants the reader to believe that production and accomplishment would cause this type of Joy and satisfy her hero's deepest longing.

This "joy in living" is further described in terms of happiness by Rand. From my understanding of the Biblical meaning of Joy, she seems to reverse the vocabulary of Joy and happiness: "joy," according to Rand, is the *feeling* of elation, while "happiness" is elation based on Reality, not mere whim or wish. This ultimate state of elation cannot come from a subjective feeling or "hallucination" that may prove false in the face of Reality; it must derive from rational Truth that cannot be refuted, or contradicted, as Rand says.

Happiness is not to be achieved at the command of emotional whims. Happiness is not the satisfaction of whatever irrational wishes you might blindly attempt to indulge. Happiness is a state of non-contradictory joy—a joy without penalty or guilt, a joy that does not clash with any of your values and does not work for your own destruction, not the joy of escaping from your mind, but of using your mind's fullest power, not the joy of faking reality, but of achieving values that are real, not the joy of a drunkard, but of a producer.[9]

When I talked to Dad about Ayn Rand's "non-contradictory joy," he took me very seriously. He knew I struggled with these questions, and he cared. He said, "I am willing to agree with her statement that 'the achievement of his own happiness is man's highest moral purpose.'"[10] He said this just after we cleared up any confusion about "if it feels good, do it." Rand argued persuasively against that. Reality comes first; what she called true "happiness" follows conditionally. The question is not whether we *seek* happiness, but what the end of that pursuit will be. Rand's way of selfishness seeks happiness in the life of the Self; the Christian pursues Joy in God. But John Piper points out, as discussed in Chapter Eight, that pursuit is, in the best sense, consummately self-interested.

[L]ove is the pursuit of our joy in the holy joy of the beloved. There is no way to exclude self-interest from love, for self-interest is not the same as selfishness. Selfishness seeks its own private happiness at the expense [or disregard] of others. Love seeks its happiness in the happiness of the beloved. It will even suffer and die for the beloved in order that its joy might be full in the life and purity of the beloved.[11]

Eclipsing our *telos*, our completion in God, is God's aim: to seek and secure His own Joy. The very foundation of Christianity—the intentional death and resurrection of Jesus Christ—has God's Joy and pleasure at its heart: "For the joy set before him, He [Jesus] endured the cross, scorning its shame, and sat down at the right hand of the throne of God."[12]

I am thrilled when I read what the Apostle Paul wrote to early Christians about God's Joy in establishing an intimate relationship with His people.

"Long, long ago he decided to adopt us into his family through Jesus Christ. (What pleasure he took in planning this!) He wanted us to enter into the celebration of his lavish gift-giving by the hand of his beloved Son."[13]

— Ephesians 1:5 (MSG)

And again, "He thought of everything, provided for everything we could possibly need, letting us in on the plans he took such delight in making. He set it all out before us in Christ, a long-range plan in which everything would be brought together and summed up in him, everything in deepest heaven, everything on planet earth."[14] Joy is woven into the fabric of the Biblical narrative. It explains God's motives, and sets a precedent. I had overlooked this for a long time.

Not only does God pursue His own Joy in Himself, but He commands His children to pursue their own Joy in Him. In the Old Testament, I encountered the worshippers' mandate to pursue joy. The Psalmist said, "Delight yourself in the Lord!"[15] That was a command to pursue Joy, in the Randian sense that it is truly in the reader's rational self-interest; and here was a prescription for how to do it!

True Joy is directly related to God and is the firm confidence that all is well, regardless of circumstances.

For the aim of the Christian Hedonist is to be happy in God, to delight in God, to cherish and enjoy His fellowship and favor. But children cannot enjoy the fellowship of their Father if He is unhappy. Therefore the foundation of Christian Hedonism is the happiness of God....

Just as our joy is based on the promise that God is strong enough and wise enough to make all things work together for our good, so God's joy is based on that same sovereign control: He makes all things work together for His glory.[16]

— John Piper

In Philippians 3:1 Paul says, "Rejoice in the Lord." The Lord is both the source and object of Christian Joy. Knowing Him brings Joy that transcends temporal circumstances. Obeying Him brings peace and assurance.

Joy is God's gift to every believer. It is the fruit that His Spirit produces from the moment a person receives the Gospel. Joy increases as when a person studies and obeys God's Word.[17]

Joy and Suffering

I see and appreciate the advent of Joy from the Biblical perspective. But I still wondered about the tragedies of life. If life with God is characterized by Joy, then what happens when tragedy strikes?

I imagined, once I became a Christian, that even trials could not withstand the Joy that now permeated my day to day. I was so full of humility, confidence, and freedom in the depth of my soul that nothing could dampen my enthusiasm for life and my appreciation of new life and Joy in knowing Jesus Christ. When difficulties did come, however, it was not what I expected.

It was more than a year since September 11, 2001, and I still hadn't found a job. The European investment bank where I had launched an equity research practice closed its U. S. Equities business. Other Wall Street firms were laying off, and it was the beginning of some tough economic times. I didn't want to leave Manhattan, but our lease was up and I had no income. An attractive start-up outside Philadelphia offered me a position, and I took it. Then, the most difficult trial of my life began.

It started in the office of a family practitioner. Navigating the bureaucracy the healthcare system—over twenty years after my initial bout with cancer—I landed in the office of more than one brain surgeon. Each explained that a tumor was resting at the base of my brain and, if we didn't do something soon, I could die. Tears began to flow.

The stress and uncertainty for my family was much more devastating that the prospect of brain surgery. The prognosis was good, and the treatments were bearable, but the side-effects were crushing. The Jesus-Joy I had come to rely on was obscured by the long, exhausting days. I couldn't sleep, I lost hearing in one ear, and I was so tired I couldn't muster the will to complain. "Where was Jesus now?" I wondered.

It was a dark time. In my darkest moments, I was stunned. The longing and the wonder at what God could possibly be doing led me to deeper contemplation. There was a lot of self-pity, but the main activity of my soul during that time was prayer, in the middle of my suffering. Through those agonizing hours, I got to know Jesus more than I ever had. It was like the friend you couldn't imagine until he sticks with you through your worst.

My friend Todd is an experienced Christian. He stands in front of every traumatic event in his life and says, "I do not know the specific reasons for this, but I know the general reasons that this is in my life. The basic business of life is to know God better. The most foundational purpose for every event, situation, and problem in my life is that I might know him better. It's the purpose and direction that everything is moving toward. While the backside of a colorful tapestry looks chaotic and messy, the right side is beautiful in its symmetry. As we are more intimately aware of the pattern beyond our circumstances, we see that they point to deeper experience and knowledge of God."

Tragedy happens, but my hope is in a living God, not in a dying world. He is "able to keep you from stumbling and to make you stand in the presence of His glory blameless with great joy."[18] The trials are key ingredients of my present Joy because of their potential to enhance my understanding and experience of Jesus, who knows me to the bottom and loves me to the top.

Joy and Knowledge

Thought would destroy their paradise. No more; where igno-rance is bliss, 'Tis folly to be wise.[19]

— Thomas Gray

If the highest endeavor for the Christian is to know God and thereby find Joy in Him, it would seem important to take up a discussion about knowledge. Even for the Objectivist pursuit of happiness, an understanding of what it is to know is significant. Knowledge is a term of comprehensive scope. We may not be able to know all things, but even the skeptic who severely limits or completely doubts Man's power to know is usually willing to admit that things beyond Man's knowledge are in themselves knowable. Simply because we have not seen certain planets or heavenly bodies doesn't mean they are invisible.

Followers of Jesus or of Ayn Rand would unite against the sentiment that ignorance is bliss. Neither believes that lack of knowledge results in happiness. What you don't know *will* hurt you. If there was a resounding theme of agreement between my two fathers, it was certainly that people should never check their brains at the door, or that "not knowing" is somehow better because it's easier on the emotions or the psyche. Dad and John would each, in his own way, remind me that knowledge and happiness are in no way mutually exclusive. Neither does one cause the other, but they relate.

In John's view, we maintain our life by our own individual effort. "That's the nature of Man and the universe: simply the way it is. The values we need—wealth and knowledge—are not given to us automatically, as a gift of nature. We have to discover them and achieve them by own individual thinking and work!" This was John's Lecture Series 101. "Happiness, or living life well, is a function of how well we discover and procure what we need and want."

Dad would have had no problem agreeing with Ayn Rand's definition: "Knowledge is a mental grasp of a fact(s) of reality, reached either by perceptual observation or by a process of reason based on perceptual observation."[20] I had come to understand that comprehension of the "facts of reality" is necessary to live, but that alone won't do the trick. The Bible talks about Knowledge as experiential and relational as in "to know someone in the Biblical sense."

The key word is Reality. It's not sufficient or even necessary to "know" something that doesn't correspond to Reality. If something can be known, it is known in the context of Reality. The question is really, "what is real?" And that gets back to a foundational question that separates the Objectivist and the Christian.

It's possible to have great intellectual knowledge and not *know*. Any parent of teenagers knows that there is a difference between knowledge that is speculative, reaching only as far as the head, and experiential knowledge. That's what the Apostle Paul was talking about when he wrote to the early church: heart knowledge. Paul prays for the early church along these lines. Apparently, he recognizes that this kind of knowledge was crucial, because he prays for this above so many other, more obvious, needs of the persecuted first-century church. After communicating his gratefulness to God in a letter to a persecuted group of believers in the Greek city of Ephesus, he writes the following:

> *I keep asking that the God of our Lord Jesus Christ, the glorious Father, may give you the Spirit of wisdom and revelation, so that you may know him better. I pray also that the eyes of your heart may be enlightened in order that you may know the hope to*

which he has called you, the riches of his glorious inheritance in the saints, and his incomparably great power for us who believe.
— Ephesians 1:17-19a (NIV)

The bottom line. Every other problem that I have can be seen as a failure to internalize, to be intimately acquainted with, an attribute of God. There's one thing I need more than anything else, and that is to know Him better. Though I may think that I need other things more urgently, the most profound and foundational thing is to know God better. Knowing God is permanent and it leads to Joy.

"Worry" could be the failure to internalize God's wisdom. I know He's wise enough to solve the problem, powerful enough to accomplish His goals, and loving enough to have my best in mind. Yet I don't know it well enough to get over my worry. Joy, I now understand, is the difference. Whether or not knowledge leads to Joy depends on the object of the knowledge. If I know lots of facts, or am loaded with experience and technical skill, these things do not determine my joy. Joy comes from God.

Objectivists can confuse the relationship between knowledge and happiness, but they are not alone in their shortcomings. I'll start with my own. The self-aggrandizing arrogance that causes me to think I am the smartest guy in the room ironically betrays a certain ignorance. The danger is not when I evaluate myself as the smartest among my peers in a given situation. That very well may be true, and there is no harm in recognizing that reality to capitalize on strengths and weaknesses. The precariousness of that first step isn't seen until later, when we embrace knowledge as our means to happiness. It gets back to idols, false gods.

When knowledge—being smart—is what gives me value, I am valuable when I meet my standard of intelligence. It's a simple equation. At the moment when I am smart, I can receive life with peace and contentment. When my intelligence falters, I'm no longer valuable. I waffle between valuing and devaluing myself, from confidence to what some would call humility.

Further, if being smart gives me value, then I will necessarily look at those who don't meet my standard of intelligence and will see others as less valuable than I am.

The universe is primarily personal, and knowledge is personal too. Life, in its most permanent form, its most meaningful form is permanent. Permanent life is only possible through knowing God, as Jesus prayed to his Father for his followers, "This is life that lasts forever. It is to know You, the only true God, and to know Jesus Christ Whom You have sent."[22]

Knowledge is Power.[21]
—Sir Francis Bacon

Knowledge is indispensable for true Joy, but how John and Dad define Joy makes the difference in the knowledge that each considers indispensable. In the same way, the linkage between knowledge and Power depends on a person's definition of Power and the ends to which he pursues it.

10

POWER

*"Did you really think that we want those laws to be ob-
served?" said Dr. Ferris. "We want them broken... We're
after power and we mean it."*[1]

— Government bureaucrat, *Atlas Shrugged*

People are obsessed with Power. Power compels us, even if it's only
ordering a cup of coffee just the way I want it. It's invigorating to control
the things that we can, though it's rare to hear someone actually confess the
thought, as Napoleon did, "Power is my mistress." Still, there's no denying
that we like to have the upper hand. As a control freak, Power is particularly
germane to me, and candidly, a lot of what I do is an attempt to control
my environment.

The discovery of my "control issues" came recently as I began discreetly telling others about my dysfunction, expecting this revelation to be as surprising to them as it was to me. No such luck! Nearly everyone who has spent more than five minutes with me can see that I have a problem. In fact, they're usually much more aware of it than I am. One morning at Starbucks, my good friend Scott disclosed this quite straightforwardly. "I like the Starbucks version of you." It was out of the blue. "I've seen the office version," he said, "and I like the Starbucks version much better. In fact, I don't want to be friends with the person I see at the office."

> For God hath not given us the spirit of fear; but of power, and of love, and of a sound mind.
>
> —2 Timothy 1:7 (KJV)

"What do you mean? What's the difference?" I was defensive, but I knew what he meant. Innocently, I waited for his answer.

"In the office, you come into the meeting with an agenda. Not in a good, organized way, but in a controlling way. Like you're going to manage everyone in the room, including what they do when they leave the meeting. You sap everyone of autonomy and not-so-subtly make them feel like children. I don't like to be managed; no one does. The Starbucks version of you doesn't do that." He called me on my not-so-hidden agenda that I try to rationalize as conviction. But to others, it is a raw exploitation of Power, overtly disguised as "just another opinion." Honestly, I don't try to discourage or undermine the intelligence and expertise in the room; it just seems to come naturally to me.

All Power is an attempt to control people, places, and things. Whether it's in the domain of a Senator or a nursery school teacher, Power can take a form either appropriate or abusive. Any given realm has its versions of how this manifests, and any given world view has its take on what Power means.

What is Power?

Despite Orwell's claim to the contrary, neither John nor Dad sees Power as an end to be sought, but more as a means to accomplish a more worthy goal.

> *Power is not a means, it is an end. One does not establish a dictatorship in order to safeguard a revolution; one makes the revolution in order to establish the dictatorship. The object of persecution is persecution. The object of torture is torture. The object of power is power.*[2]

The word "power" derives from the old French word "poeir," which means "to be able to act." Power is the ability or capacity to perform or act effectively, including the situation where not to act is most effective. In democracies, Power is typically divided against itself for the purpose of balance: the classic tripartite division of Power in legislative, executive, and judicial branches. In contemporary, pluralistic democracies the divisions of Power go much further; and it is not limited to the arena of formal politics. Issues of Power pertain to markets, technologies, science, discourses, designs, fashions, and self-improvement. The result is that "Power is everywhere."

In *Atlas Shrugged*, Ayn Rand displays the real driver behind the success of the entire economic, social, and political world: the human mind. The rational mind can accomplish great things. However, according to Rand, people throw their weight around, in right ways and wrong ones. Whether mystics of spirit or mystics of muscle, those who leave the realm of the mind are abusers of Power. They achieve their goals through Force, a false use of Power. Rand articulated that the uninitiated use of Force always leads to problems. The abusers of power, the users of uninitiated physical force, are always in the wrong. "Uninitiated" includes those who take their guns or other physical means and compel others to do their will. That was the case when Rearden's mills were destroyed by the rioters. The governmental establishment had no rational way to defeat Rearden's choice to produce his innovative metal on his own terms. Instead of appealing to Reason, to Man's mind and the logic that determines what is right, they forced their agenda by hiring thugs to incite a riot in his mills. In so doing, the mystics of force made it appear that Rearden was the perpetrator of oppression in his ruthless demands on those who worked in the mills. This was far from the case.

> *Every Communist must grasp the truth, "Political power grows out of the barrel of a gun."*[3]
>
> — Mao Tse-tung

Ayn Rand said, "There are only two means by which men can deal with one another: guns or logic. Force or persuasion. Those who know they cannot win by means of logic, have always resorted to guns."[4] While Rand maintained that morality is the greatest of all intellectual capacities, she understood that most of the Power exercised in today's world is through coercion. In her writing, the mystics of muscle were Soviet Russia and Nazi Germany. Because morality is as necessary as philosophy, so Rand's Attila in all ages will look for morality. Since the morality of the mind is inconsistent with force as a means of Power, the only morality left is the morality of death: that which places Faith above Reason, revelation above observation.

Atlas Shrugged describes a world where the government wields ever-increasing Power, a world controlled by those who preach Altruism in the guise of "fairness for all." They act out of deceit. They claim to have "the public good" in mind, yet their endgame is trickery to take for themselves. James Taggart is arguably the most hypocritical of all Ayn Rand's characters. His plea for the good of the many serves as an elaborate cloak to cover his own inexhaustible desire for Power at the expense of everything else.

Government's Rightful Role

In *Atlas Shrugged*, as in Rand's own day, she viewed a government that was overreaching its intended role. This is the most obvious abuse of Power Rand objects to. Both Dad and John agree that she makes a good case for "limited government." She was by no means an anarchist; she articulates a clear role for government: to protect its citizens from criminals at home and abroad.

Rand observed the United States government abandoned its rightful role when she was alive. Since that time, it has expanded its size and influence in the lives of individuals. As she articulated in her fiction and nonfiction, I think Rand would have seen the government's increasing regulation of free markets, its continued seizing of private property, and its redistribution of wealth as trends toward Socialism that would lead to the Communism she fled in the early twentieth century. As the government becomes more of a benefactor to individuals and groups, we will necessarily see fewer decisions being made by individuals. With decision making comes control. More government control diminishes individual liberty. What follows is unavoidable. As the government controls more and more aspects of our lives, it abuses the Power entrusted to it. And most pernicious, it does this under the guise of protecting the very citizens it is systematically disempowering with its mandates.

The Public Choice economists remind us that contrary to what the civics textbooks imply, public "servants" have the same ambitions as the rest of us — wealth, career, influence, prestige. But there's a big difference between us and them. Politicians, bureaucrats and the people they "rescue" get money through force—taxation. Don't think taxation is force? Try not paying, and see what happens.

The rest of us must achieve our goals through voluntary
exchange in the marketplace. That difference—force versus vol-
untary exchange—makes all the difference in the world.[5]

— John Stossel

Manipulation

Power, in the context of these discussions, is best characterized as "manipulation." Manipulation is a non-physical form of what Ayn Rand calls "brute
force." In prior chapters I have cited Rand's disdain for the perversion of
Power. As a prime example, she cites the Witch Doctor's use of Faith to
manipulate.

The essential characteristics of these two [the man of faith
and the man of force] remain the same in all ages: Attila, the man
who rules by brute force, acts on the range of the moment, is con-
cerned with nothing but the physical reality immediately before
him, respects nothing but man's muscles, and regards a fist, a
club or a gun as the only answer to any problem—and the Witch
Doctor, the man who dreads physical reality, dreads the necessity
of practical action, and escapes into his emotions, into visions of
some mystic realm where his wishes enjoy a supernatural power
unlimited by the absolute of nature.[6]

When truth claims appeal to or imply an authority that one party
cannot question or criticize, but must accept without question, the discussion is over. That's how Rand characterizes Faith. Put aside for a moment
that she rejects Faith as a means of knowledge. She dismisses Christianity as
"mystic," because mysticism rejects the objective in favor of Faith, of revelation; it rejects proof and offers no evidence.

In Rand's linking of Force and Faith, she sees the Power of one as the outgrowth of the other. As she describes it,

the one who survives by Force—taking (instead of producing)
what he needs to sustain his life—operates without a philosoph-
ical code of values to guide his choices and actions.

If he understood that his mind were his means of survival, he would not be looting the production of others. Acting contrary to Man's nature, he is often struck with a sense of guilt and uncertainty because he has no integrated view of life that allows him to continue his existence. In the absence of Reason, there is nothing left but arbitrary consciousness, or Faith.

Among others, the most chilling mystics of spirit today are Islamic fundamentalists, manipulators who feed the morality of death to those who will use force to compel allegiance. After September 11, 2001, many people fervently wrote that religious fundamentalism is the cause of the world's evil and violence. The argument goes, "When people insist on absolute truth, through a revelation from some higher power, that cannot be debated, it ends in oppression and terrorist acts." Kathy Keller rightly rejected this line of observation as too general. She pointed out that it depends on the fundamental. "Amish are fundamentalists. When is the last time you saw an Amish terrorist?"[7] Dogmatic overreaches notwithstanding, commitment to fundamentals in and of itself need not mean abuse of Power, much less adherence to destructive force.

Wherefore if a man, in self-defense, uses more than neces-
sary violence, it will be unlawful: whereas if he repel force with
moderation his defense will be lawful, because according to the
jurists ... "it is lawful to repel force by force, provided one does
not exceed the limits of a blameless defense."[8]

— Thomas Aquinas

177

It can be properly said that Rand, herself, was a "fundamentalist," and her fundamentalism was the principle that the individual embrace a rational morality of self-interest.

The Abuse of Power

To force a man to drop his own mind and to accept your will as a substitute, with a gun in place of a syllogism, with terror in place of proof, and death as the final argument—is to attempt to exist in defiance of reality. Reality demands of man that he act for his own rational interest; your gun demands of him that he act against it. Reality threatens man with death if he does not act on his rational judgment: you threaten him with death if he does. You place him into a world where the price of his life is the surrender of all the virtues required by life—and death by a process of gradual destruction is all that you and your system will achieve, when death is made to be the ruling power, the winning argument in a society of men.[9]

— John Galt

All violence consists in some people forcing others, under threat of suffering or death, to do what they do not want to do.[10]

— *Leo Tolstoy*

The abuse of Power always seems to bring with it the arrogance of claimed superiority. The claim is explicit when one individual or group looks down on others because they are "without the truth" or they do not achieve "success" by whatever definition. Alternatively, the claim to superiority is implicit when one group thinks nothing of the other, when it is not even recognized.

Where any institution or a world view prescribes standards of behavior or thought, there will be a conflict between confidence and humility. If

I meet the standards, then I can be confident, but my confidence will tend toward arrogance rather than humility. I will look down on others who are not meeting the standard, because I consider that standard is entirely within their grasp. A person looking down on someone else says, "Hey, I am living proof that this can be done, this standard can be met. Buck up! Get with the program."

This sense of superiority applies more to Rand's philosophy than to the Gospel—not because of the tone or demeanor of her arguments—but because of their content. Namely, Rand presents a standard that excludes non-adherents on the basis of their performance. Similarly, the Gospel insists on an equally high (or higher) standard and excludes non-adherents on the basis of performance. In the Gospel, however, the individual benefits from the performance of Christ, who alone meets the standard on his behalf, making confidence and humility possible simultaneously.

One view of the church prevalent in Western culture today is that Christianity is not dedicated to serving the truth; rather it is intent on accruing and maintaining institutional power. The history of the church, tragically, includes its own share of Power abuse. Is it unavoidable? Do the Christian's truth claims lead inevitably to abusive Power? I would assert the opposite, that the tenets of Gospel Faith are the best guards against the misuse of Power. Yet there is no denying some notable examples. Clergy sex-abuse scandals continue to send shock waves throughout the Roman Catholic Church, year after year. Churches like the Boston Church of Christ are exposed for their methods of controlling all aspects of their members' lives, from finances to marriage. More subtle abuse of authority in the church leads to shaming and exiling people in ways that have no grounding in Scripture; and "spiritual abuse" has become a topic for recovery groups as well as a category in Christian publishing.

Truth Claims as a Means to Power

What we know, and how we assert what we know can often translate to Power. Francis Bacon's axiom is perennially verifiable: knowledge *is* Power. Truth claims are a means to control, a way to wield Power. The Power in a truth claim derives from a prescribed way to live that flows from an understanding of Reality. If I claim a truth that is irrelevant to the way you think or live, no Power accrues to me. But if what I say is true necessitates thoughts or actions on your part, then I exert tremendous Power over you. I am telling you what to do. Even if I don't see Power as an end in itself, I maintain that truth claims are acutely relevant to everyday thoughts and behaviors.

Here is an example. The scene is the last play of a backyard football game. The team is down by three points, with only one play to make the difference. The players are worn out and weary, but Billy stands up in the huddle and says, "I have a plan to win the game." This is Billy's truth claim. Without time to hear the merits of his plan and be persuaded, the team must either cede Power to him by blindly following what he says, or face the alternative.

Not everyone maintains that truth claims are valid. Disciples of the twentieth-century French philosopher, Michel Foucault, for instance, condemn both Christianity and Randian thought on the basis that truth claims are merely a bid for Power. Doing so, however, they also condemn themselves on their own terms. Tim Keller addresses Foucault's influence in this regard.

> *The French philosopher Foucault writes: "Truth is a thing of this world. It is produced only by multiple forms of constraint and that includes the regular effects of power." Inspired by Foucault, many say that all truth-claims are power plays. When you claim to have the truth, you are trying to get power and control over other people.*[11]

Those who don't believe in moral absolutes often point to this idea to invalidate them. If someone is making a claim, then they are doing it to gain some form of Power. For example, if I claimed "everyone should give to those in need" in front of Nietzsche, he would question whether I said that because I really felt compassion or because I wanted to start a revolution that would give me control and Power. If, as the relativist believes, there is no absolute truth, then my claim of exclusive knowledge of the truth must be false. If I do not know it is false, I am merely deluded and pitiable. If I know it is false, I am a deceiver and almost certainly motivated by money, Power, or some other derivation of the same.

Since both Objectivism and Christianity make absolute truth claims, they have been widely disregarded. Using Foucault's own logic, however, we can actually discount that claim. The statement "All truth claims are a bid for Power" is itself a bid for Power and can be dismissed.

We don't accept all such assertions without discrimination, but we shouldn't throw them all out indiscriminately, either. How do we discern whether a truth claim is a bid for Power? For anyone making a truth claim, his motivation is revealed by his *use* of Power. I've seen my share of Objectivists and Christians, and frankly, their lives by no means consistently indicate the underlying truth of either world view. Moreover, both Objectivism and Christianity make truth claims that exclude assertions outside of themselves. Yet, even if the lives of their adherents offer some of the best evidence against their assertions, observing those lives can offer compelling validations of such truth claims. All of this leads to a necessary and healthy consideration of the truth claims themselves. For that, we must consider what each world view actually says, regardless of how well it's interpreted and applied.

The Power of the Objectivist's Truth Claims

"We never make assertions, Miss Taggart," said Hugh Akston. "That is the moral crime peculiar to our enemies. We do not tell—we show. We do not claim—we prove."[12]

Rand's heroes don't go after Power for its own sake. Following the behaviors that Rand advocates does not signal allegiance to her per se, but allegiance of the individual to his own mind and Reason. The true end of Man is living according to the nature of Man, using his mind. The outgrowth of using one's mind is always creating value, producing. Rand says that an individual must produce everything that is necessary to sustain a "life well lived," one's own happiness. By her standards, the way I relate to others is not lording something over them with Power based on a truth claim. Rather, it's by trading the value that I have produced for an equal value of what another has produced. My value as a person derives from my ability to produce that which is valuable. According to Rand, so does yours.

In John's understanding of Reality, human beings have no choice of survival methods. He unpacked it for me. "First, I choose to live," he said. "It sounds obvious, but it's an act of the will." He continued, "Then, I use my mind to produce what is necessary to sustain my life. Doing it well is the key." He smiled knowingly. When he did that, I sometimes felt that he was reading my mind, like he knew how I thought about what he said.

He was talking about Rand's "non-contradictory joy" or "the reward and consequence of successful action."[13] If Rand's characters are the proto-type, anyone will be successful and happy to the degree that he "gets" and applies this understanding of Reality.

Those who "get it" are the producers. The producers are the "haves" and the non-producers are the "have-nots." Importantly, they have because they produce what they have. Production comes first; it's not a result of some privileged position of wealth or the "aristocracy of pull," in which a person's connections determine the behavior of those around him. The quality and standard of what is produced determines the value that accrues to the producer. Furthermore, whether or not I am a producer dictates how I view myself. If I produce a particular standard of behavior, then I can have the confidence and authority and the Power that comes with that. If I do not produce, then by definition, I cannot but question my value as a person. Absent the use of brute force, I am left with no alternative than to subjugate myself to the producer. According to Rand, if I have the mind to produce, I am able to validate and demonstrate my value.

> *The motors were a moral code cast in steel.*
> *They are alive, she thought, because they are the physical shape of the action of a living power—of the mind that had been able to grasp the whole of this complexity, to set its purpose, to give it form.[14]*

I've had this view for most of my life. My ability to get things done, my professional success, my accomplished Ivy League career—all of it validates my sound choices. It all seemed within my control. The operative word is "seemed." That was the "little white lie" that kept me guessing. In truth, the vast majority of my life has been outside of my control: cancer at the age of sixteen, crippling side effects, out of work at several junctures in my adult life. All of these are stones in a dilapidated fortress that is ravaged by the artillery of life's many battles. Still, from Rand's perspective, even these beyond-my-control trials afford an opportunity to survive and produce using Reason to overcome life's inevitable challenges.

Since my individual value is entirely dependent on my behavior as a producer or a non-producer, whether I am a producer or a non-producer is entirely defined by my behavior. Distorting Hamlet, "To produce or not to produce, that determines my value." Put another way, I can receive life with joy and peace if I am a producer of value. If not, I cannot.

If I produce, it's because *I* do it; I *choose* to do it; it's within my control. In Rand's philosophy, anyone may choose not to produce, as he wishes, but he can't, as a consequence, respect himself as someone who does produce. By Rand's definition, he has less worth than a producer. He is less valuable. That conclusion leads to some dangerous ground.

It seems a psychological necessity to look down on someone who doesn't live up to the standard by which I validate my own worth as a person. If I pride myself on being an industrious person—if production and industry become my value-defining quality—then I will bristle when I see someone who is a non-producer, who is irrational, or lazy. I'll look down on him because the choice to be lazy is his. I am a producer and he is *not*.

This kind of differentiation manifests negatively in the way we view people who come to different conclusions. Keller characterizes this propensity with Postmodernism in particular; though I think it has always been the inclination of people to exclude.

> *Postmodern thinkers understand that the self is formed and strengthened through the exclusion of the Other—those who do not have the values or traits on which I base my own significance. We define ourselves by pointing to those whom we are not. We bolster our sense of worth by devaluing those of other races, beliefs, and traits.*[15]

Like the proverbial frog in the frying pan, the burning sense of alienation doesn't happen all at once. First we disassociate ourselves from those who don't "get it." Then we rationalize that we have less in common with them, and eventually, that we are better. It's easier to criticize characteristics and behavior than to address human beings as inferior, but the result is the same: the abuse of Power, leading to oppression, war, and injustice.

The Power of the Christian's Truth Claims

Christianity, in its purest form, views Power differently. There is a certain anti-power that comes from the Gospel, typified in the seemingly contradictory statement, "but many that are first shall be last and the last shall be first."[16] What is confusing and even intellectually scandalous to people about the Gospel really comes down to Power. The great paradox of Christianity is that Jesus gave up Power, or apparently gave it up, to foil the counterfeit power of the Devil and to put an end to the Power of sin and death.

> *What is confusing and even intellectually scandalous to people about the Gospel really comes down to Power.*

The uniqueness of the Christian perspective on Power hit me when I studied the life of Paul the Apostle. A renowned German scholar said this of him: "There is no single person since Nero's days who has left such permanent marks on the souls of men as Paul the New Man." He saw the Apostle Paul "rising from the mass of the insignificant many" and "still molding the world at the present moment."[17] Here is a man with a superlative pedigree as a first-century Jewish religious leader. He spoke at least three languages, was formally educated, and well-read in contemporary culture and politics. I would expect someone of his caliber to feel quite prepared for the task of getting the word out about Jesus. Instead of emphasizing his résumé, however, he continually underscored his shortcomings—not an effective interview tactic, if you ask me.

In a letter to the first-century church in Corinth, Paul described some of his weaknesses with frankness, even boldness and vulnerability. He confided that he had prayed for healing, but that God had not healed him. His response?

> *Now I take limitations in stride, and with good cheer, these limitations that cut me down to size—abuse, accidents, opposition, bad breaks. I just let Christ take over! And so the weaker I get, the stronger I become.*
>
> — 2 Corinthians 12:9-10 (MSG)

With confidence and humility, the Apostle Paul was able to achieve more in a few years than most historical figures have achieved in a lifetime. And he attributes that success to a Power that operates in the realm of the unseen.

To be fair, most of the Power we've been describing in this chapter is not observable in the conventional sense, unless it's physical force. Power operates in the psychological realm. But Paul extends his understanding of Power to another realm altogether.

Like the Apostle Paul, the Christian is imbued with the Power of the Holy Spirit. Wrongly understood (like Rand's misinterpretation of Sacrifice), the Christian is weak, insipid, powerless—hence the contempt of thinkers like Nietzsche and Rand. But rightly comprehended and engaged in, the Christian life is one characterized by the Power of God. The Bible brings all the language of triumphant warfare to bear in its description of the Christian life. The promise of the New Testament in particular is that these are not mere metaphors, but through the transformation of minds, people can be empowered spiritually in ways that change lives! Here may be exactly where John's mystic meter would jump off its dial; yet the hard, empirical evidence throughout the history of Christendom of people healed, relationships restored, addictions overcome, difficulties endured with joy... should speak loudly to the rational assessor.

As I have certainly become convinced, there is a distinct difference between the Christian Gospel and what most people consider "religion." Rand's antagonists are far more like the religious Pharisees of the first century, twisting Power to their own ends; whereas those who base their lives on the Gospel exhibit more of the self-assuredness of Randian heroes. The extent to which Christians in any era are acting in line with the Gospel is the extent to which they balance the characteristics of circumspect confidence and appropriate self-awareness.

When my own personal grasp of the gospel was very weak, my self-view swung wildly between two poles. When I was performing up to my standards—in academic work, professional achievement, or relationships—I felt confident but not humble. I was likely to be proud and unsympathetic to failing people. When I was not living up to standards, I felt humble but not confident, a failure. I discovered, however, that the gospel contained the resources to build a unique identity. In Christ I could know I was accepted by grace not only despite my flaws, but because I was willing to admit them. The Christian gospel is that I am so flawed that Jesus had to die for me, yet I am so loved and valued that Jesus was glad to die for me. This leads to deep humility and deep confidence at the same time. It undermines both swaggering and sniveling. I cannot feel superior to anyone, and yet I have nothing to prove to anyone. I do not think more of myself nor less of myself. Instead I think of myself less.[18]

— Timothy J. Keller

Thinking that is in line with the Christian Gospel brings about a new perspective on people who don't believe like I do or look like I do. This thinking engenders inclusiveness, because everyone comes to God with nothing. In fact, nothing is *exactly* what everyone comes with, and if he comes with more, God refuses him. It gets back to the Power issue. If I come to God with anything that asserts a claim, then He owes me. Instead, God has done everything for me because I was unable to do it for myself. Throwing myself on Him for mercy, He chose to come through. Now I owe Him everything.

The Gospel substantially re-orders how one gains and exhibits Power. It frees the believer from putting too much hope or meaning in things that are at best penultimate goods, like Sex, Money, and Power. In other words, these things are all demoted in life. Remember, works-based religion is

"I perform, therefore I'm acceptable;" the Gospel is "I am accepted through Jesus Christ, therefore I perform." These are two radically different motivations for living. If people operate on the religious principle, they have to find something they do or something they have that enables them to feel they're worthwhile, that they're significant and secure. The need for significance drives us to give Power to status, relationships, and accomplishments to define our worth.

Yet, the Apostle Paul says that the Gospel defines Christ's disciples as the new people of God who will inherit the new heavens and the new earth. With that as my destiny, I am freed from giving consummate Power to any present aspect of my life. I *partake* in the bounty of this life. I find happiness and delight in my relationships and my work; but I no longer characterize or achieve my ultimate purpose or validation from them. I am empowered by God to use the very qualities that had once defined me for other purposes. Instead of meeting my needs alone, Money, Sex, and Power are employed to build human community and Christian community.

By yielding to a Power greater than myself, I have gained a new Power.

Conclusion

Whether subtle or overt, the effects of Power manifest in every strata of society. The benefits as well as the machinations of Power have been experienced in every era of recorded human history: kingdoms prosper and grow; lives are twisted and brought to ruin. We can live in denial about it, but Power operates always and everywhere in some way or another; and as with other issues that are significantly colored by our world views, it is important to recognize where and how it functions in our lives. Only by knowing this do we respond to Power in our best interest and use Power responsibly.

As I plumbed the depths of Rand's thought, I became increasingly convinced that Power accrues to producers. Among the people whom

I respected growing up—my family and my community—producers were "on the inside." That was where I wanted to be. Sometimes I felt securely part of that family when I lived up to or acquiesced to the standard. Other times, I felt alienated and looked down upon. Regardless of the intentions of my parents, those were my feelings. While Rand may not have envisioned alienating the "have nots," it seemed the inevitable conclusion of her logic.

On the other hand, I saw the Christian community—a new family of sorts—that was voluntarily giving up its Power to empower others. I studied the impact of Christians on the Roman Empire in the first century, the British Empire during the Great Awakening, and America during the Second Great Awakening, bringing millions of people into a peace and Joy that they had never known, transforming society, running through rich and poor communities alike. This was the Christianity I wanted. Not a narrow, religious, guilt-producing club that may provide comfort or a crutch during hard times. That couldn't be the same Christianity that transformed Empires!

The more I understood Jesus, his Power to transform, and the mission that swept me into something so much bigger than myself, the more I wanted to give up my small ambitions for something that was more true, more challenging, and more fulfilling than what I had ever dreamed possible: much, much more.

Part III

FRUITS OF CONVERSATION:

THE DESTINATION

11

WHO IS JOHN GALT? REALLY

The opening line of *Atlas Shrugged* "Who is John Galt?" becomes an expression of helplessness and despair in the current state of the novel's fictionalized world. Before finding the real John Galt, Dagny Taggart hears various legends about Galt. After eventually joining his cause, she learns that all of the stories contain an element of truth. Rand's entire view of the world is summed up in her ideal man.

Son of a blue-collar worker from an insubstantial locale, his childhood is obscure, as is his family. In his youth, his teachers view him as their most promising pupil. As he grows, he embarks on a mission to right the world. Gradually, people begin to see what he can do, but he stays in the shadows until the timing is right. While he eventually attracts many followers, his genius is initially exposed to only a small group in a remote place.

He is the ideal man, a heroic being, with intelligence, charisma, and integrity; his character is immutable. He understands and articulates wisdom that resonates with a certain type of person who is prepared to hear it. He persuades people individually and goes after those he chooses, steadily, patiently, and with passion and perseverance. He prepares a place for a select few, and all who go there would rather be no place else. Despite this, he is treated like a common criminal, even worse. He is tortured for his virtue, more so than any other hero.

He came with the answer to the world's ills, and he spoke with Reason, but his message was not understood. He was rejected. More than that, his detractors viewed his "wisdom" as folly, and considered him to be the problem, not the answer. His enemies tried to bribe him, offered him any-thing he wished, to become part of their plan. He refused. He was prepared to die for his true love. He was complicit in his own torture, and his enemies plotted his humiliation, all while they despised his true mission.

Not-So-Ominous Parallels

Who is this? For those unfamiliar with Ayn Rand's epic hero, it would be easy to mistake the description of John Galt for Jesus Christ. The parallels are unmistakable. As I have considered the similarities, it seems unlikely that that this is a coincidence. But it is jarring, given Rand's hostility toward Christianity. Why would she build a hero so obviously evocative of a world view she loathed!

Salvador Dali painted *Crucifixion (Corpus Hypercubus)* in 1954. It depicts Jesus being crucified on the net of a hypercube. I became familiar with Dali—and this oil on canvas—long before I learned that it was Ayn Rand's favorite painting. In Jeff Britting's book, *Ayn Rand*, he writes that she felt "a kinship between her personal view of John Galt's defiance over his torture in *Atlas Shrugged* and Dali's depiction of the suffering of Jesus."[1]

Rand saw the resemblance between Dali's painting and the scene in which John Galt rises above his torturers, even as they run screaming from what he has made them realize about themselves. Perhaps the creed of the independent man, from Rand's *Anthem*, serves as the text.

> *I stand here on the summit of the mountain. I lift my head and I spread my arms. This, my body and spirit, this is the end of the quest. I wished to know the meaning of things. I am the meaning. I wished to find a warrant for being. I need no warrant for being, and no word of sanction upon my being. I am the warrant and the sanction.*[2]

Apparently Rand would stare at this painting of Jesus for hours.

> *Are you beginning to see who is John Galt? I am the man who has earned the thing you did not fight for, the thing you have renounced, betrayed, corrupted, yet were unable fully to destroy and are now hiding as your guilty secret... you still long to say what I am now saying to the hearing of the whole of mankind: I am proud of my own value and of the fact that I wish to live.*[3]
>
> — John Galt

Throughout history, there have been allusions to heroes who provide moral examples of the way we should live. Sometimes they move us to take risks, inspire us to pursue an ideal, and challenge us to realize our highest potential. As Leonard Peikoff writes, John Galt gives us that kind of hero.

> *According to the Objectivist esthetics, a crucial purpose of art is to depict man as he might be and ought to be, and thereby provide the reader or viewer with the pleasure of contemplating, in concrete, embodied form, his abstract moral ideal. Howard Roark*

and John Galt provide this kind of inspiration to me, and to many other people I know.[4]

At the risk of his own life, John Galt endured torture to rescue his beloved. True to his knowledge of Reality, he resisted the enticements of his enemies; his unwillingness to cooperate foiled their plans. The inspiration of John Galt challenges us to become the best possible version of ourselves: the ideal man.

Above everything else, it presented my ideal man fully. I can never surpass Galt. More than that, I now have four variants: Roark, Galt, Rearden, and Francisco. There is no point in multiplying them. What worries me about my future in fiction is that the motor of my interest—the presentation of the ideal man and the ideal way of life—is gone.[5]

Ayn Rand considered her portrayal of the ideal man to be complete. Without question, I am moved by these themes. Yet, if the exhortation to "go back into the world and do likewise" is the last word, I am left wanting. At the end of the day, there must be something more.

Jesus, the True John Galt

Indeed, there is more. There is One who is an even greater "John Galt" than Rand's hero. The True John Galt not only put His life at risk to stop the world's headlong plunge to its own destruction, but in the face of certain death, He engaged. He endured torture in order not to lose the ones He came to the world to save. And He did this "for the joy set before him."[6]

John Galt's moral example sets a high standard that few can achieve. Yet the example of Jesus is so far out of reach that no one can achieve it. Knowing this from the beginning, Jesus not only became our Example; He became our Substitute, meeting the standard on our behalf.

Galt is Rand's example of "the best within us."[7] Watching him live shows us how to think about our own life in light of Reality. Not only does Jesus show us true humanity, He also gives us the power to live out that life in vital relationship with the One who designed us and has a vision for our Joy.

When you understand that Jesus is not only the Ideal Man, but that He is the One who brings us to Joy, all of the good things in your life will pale in comparison to His surpassing greatness. In the way that Augustine proposes, your "loves" will be ordered.[8] Tim Keller puts that experience into practical terms when he writes,

> *Galt is Rand's example of "the best within us." Watching him live shows us how to think about our own life in light of Reality.*

> *Does it move you to think of what Jesus did for you? When that begins to really move you, amaze you, make you weep, you'll have a fighting chance of avoiding the trap. Letting Jesus's sacrifice melt you will drain money of its importance for you. Human status becomes just human status. Approval becomes just approval. You can give money away or you can keep it, depending on what's the best thing at the time. The only way I know to counteract the power of money in your life is to see the ultimate Rich Young Ruler, who gave away everything to come after you, to rescue you, to love you.[9]*

Rand's Atlas

In Greek mythology, Atlas was the Titan condemned to hold up the heavens on his shoulders. According to Plato, Atlas was the first king of Atlantis, which, as it happens, is another name for the utopian society set up by John Galt. To observe Atlas is to see who or what sustains the world. My favorite depiction of Atlas is one that Rand, living on the East Side, would have seen during her New York years: a fifteen-foot, bronze statue in front of Rockefeller Center. Atlas holds the heavens as high as a four-story building.

> *If you saw Atlas, the giant who holds the world on his shoulders, if you saw that he stood, blood running down his chest, his knees buckling, his arms trembling but still trying to hold the world aloft with the last of this strength, and the greater his effort the heavier the world bore down on his shoulders—what would you tell him to do?*[10]
>
> — Francisco D'Anconia

Rand pictures the producers supporting the world: holding it up by the strength of their minds. The increasing burden of the producers is compounded by the world's decreasing appreciation, or even recognition, of their effort. As the story of *Atlas Shrugged* develops, Rand paints a picture of the producers—acting on their own reasoning and under the leadership of John Galt—refusing to be victimized, refusing to suffer for "doing good." The world simply will not listen to the reasonable pleas of Rand's heroes. Society deteriorates, morality declines, and the economic woes crush, it seems, the very soul of America. As the situation worsens, creating value becomes increasingly more difficult. The producers cannot continue to support the world that—out of stubbornness or ignorance—refuses to see. Who can blame Atlas for shrugging in the face of such inane circumstances, for throwing off the world in violent indifference? In a quasi-version of *Left Behind* for atheists, the producers strike, and the world topples with no one to sustain it.[11]

Jesus, the True Atlas

Jesus also faced unfathomable depths of suffering. Unlike Rand's villains, Jesus in no way embraced suffering for its own sake, as a virtue in itself. He did not crave death, and He especially dreaded the separation from God of which death was a small part. The eighteenth-century revivalist Jonathan Edwards inspired his hearers when he preached a sermon entitled, "Christ's Agony." He envisioned the inner turmoil that Christ must have undergone as He considered the heinous death that lay ahead of Him.

> *The strength of Christ's love more especially appears in this, that when he had such a full view of the dreadfulness of the cup that he was to drink, that so amazed him, he would notwithstanding even then take it up, and drink it. Then seems to have been the greatest and most peculiar trial of the strength of the love of Christ, when God set down the bitter portion before him, and let him see what he had to drink, if he persisted in his love to sinners; and brought him to the mouth of the furnace that he might see its fierceness, and have a full view of it, and have time then to consider whether he would go in and suffer the flames of this furnace for such unworthy creatures, or not... Will you cast yourself into this dreadful furnace of wrath?"[12]*

The fierceness that Edwards describes is truly awesome; he creates a powerful scene wherein we enter the Jesus's dilemma. Will He stay and bear the suffering for the sake of those who do not appreciate and cannot even understand—whether out of stubbornness or ignorance—what in the world He is doing?

In comparison to Francisco's words about Atlas's agony, the anguish of Jesus seems exorbitant. It was. Edwards portrays the tension of this dilemma through an imagined inner dialogue of Jesus.

> *Why should I, who have been living from all eternity in the enjoyment of the Father's love, go to cast myself into such a furnace for them that never can requite me for it? Why should I yield myself to be thus crushed by the weight of divine wrath, for them who have no love to me, and are my enemies?... Such, however,*

was not the language of Christ's heart; in these circumstances;
but on the contrary, his love held out, and he resolved even then,
in the midst of his agony, to yield himself up to the will of God, and
to take the cup and drink it.[13]

Jesus did yield Himself in love. He took up the cross and was crucified. And with the image of Jesus carrying the cross, I hearken back to the statue of Atlas on Fifth Avenue, where there is a poignant contrast. Across the street from Atlas stands the majestic Saint Patrick's Cathedral. There, facing one another, these monuments pay tribute to the world views of my fathers: Christianity and Objectivism; Faith and Reason. Each is resolute in its position and stands in strength. Yet, they could not be more disparate. Where Atlas carries the world, Jesus carries the cross. Atlas is a muscular, godlike Titan; Jesus's broken body makes Him look frail and feeble. Where Atlas is a symbol of strength, Jesus's strength comes out of his weakness. Where Atlas refuses to suffer and abandons the world, Jesus does something altogether different. The significance of His suffering is more profound, and consequently more moving than I had ever imagined. Instead of weakly accepting the world's ill-treatment as a victim, He intentionally lays down his life for the world. In so doing, He redeems the world from the sin and alienation at the heart of the problem. I used to think that Jesus simply continued to bleed as a symbol of suffering for the sake of suffering, that He simply continued in order to be an example of martyrdom. If that were all, it would be a rather warped and pointless symbol.

Where Atlas carries the world, Jesus carries the cross.

Jonathan Edwards continues the description in the same message.

For though his sufferings were greater afterwards, when he
was on the cross, yet he saw clearly what those sufferings were
to be, in the time of his agony; ... His human nature had been in a

struggle with his love to sinners, but his love had got the victory.
The thing, upon a full view of his sufferings, had been resolved
on and concluded; and accordingly, when the moment arrived, he
actually went through with those sufferings.[14]

Dagny's Longing

In her literary genius, Rand foreshadows John Galt as Dagny's romantic,
philosophical, and heroic partner. Long before she meets him, she yearns.

> *It was only in the first few years that she felt herself screaming*
> *silently, at times, for a glimpse of human ability, a single glimpse of*
> *clean, hard, radiant competence. She had fits of tortured longing*
> *for a friend or an enemy with a mind better than her own. But the*
> *longing passed.*[15]

Interestingly, for most of Dagny's life, her longing found its outlet in
work: the productive capacity in herself or in others. Later, when she con-
templates building the John Galt Line as a rebellious gesture to the apathy
and ineptitude she despises, she considers that her longing may be embodied
in something that is not less than production, but much, much more.

> *This was a longing she had never permitted herself to*
> *acknowledge. She faced it now. She thought: To find a feeling that*
> *would hold, as their sum, as their final expression, the purpose of*
> *all the things she loved on earth... To find a consciousness like*
> *her own, who would be the meaning of her world, as she would be*
> *of his... A man who existed only in her knowledge of her capacity*
> *for an emotion she had never felt, but would have given her life*
> *to experience... She twisted herself in a slow, faint movement, her*
> *breasts pressed to the desk; she felt the longing in her muscles, in*
> *the nerves of her body.*[16]

Dagny's longing was for what she knew, deep inside, to be the reason for her existence: the competence that defined an authentic individual, a man or woman of Reason. And Rand illustrates the fulfillment of that longing in a person. John Galt is the hero Dagny longs for, and heaven is finding him. Dagny's desire is not only normal, it is expected from a rational individual seeking values that will promote her own life. And she is a rational being: one who survives and thrives through Reason.

> Our commonest expedient is to call it beauty and behave as if that had settled the matter....
>
> — C. S. Lewis

While I learned about the concept of "longing" from *Atlas Shrugged*, it was theoretical until I read one of Dad's favorite authors, C. S. Lewis. Lewis was a contemporary of Rand's, but they moved in different circles, as most Christians and Objectivists do today. While he wrote prior to Ayn Rand, it seemed like she could have written some of his radio talks or public speeches.

Reading *Atlas Shrugged*, it was like Rand had discovered a secret yearning of my own. Lewis describes something of what that felt like.

We all experience what Lewis refers to as

> *a desire for something that has never actually appeared in our experience. We cannot hide it because our experience is constantly suggesting it, and we betray ourselves like lovers at the mention of a name. Our commonest expedient is to call it beauty and behave as if that had settled the matter.... The books or the music in which we thought the beauty was located will betray us if we trust to them; it was not in them, it only came through them, and what came through them was longing.*[17]

Lewis nearly describes the depths of my soul's longing: so palpable, it's like "the scent of a flower we have not picked, the echo of a tune we have not heard, news from a country we have not yet visited." I was struck by his

emotive description of this "longing." Rand alludes to the emotional aspect
as well when Dagny admits her feelings of longing to the men she admires
in the valley of Galt's Gulch. Ken Danagger aptly describes what she would
want from great men, were she to meet them in heaven.

> *"There's something you'd want to hear from them. I didn't
> know it, either, until I saw him for the first time"—he pointed to
> Galt—"and he said it to me, and then I knew what it was that
> I had missed all my life. Miss Taggart, you'd want them to look at
> you and to say, 'Well done.'"* She dropped her head and nodded
> silently, head down, not to let him see the sudden spurt of tears to
> her eyes.[18]

All Rand had to do was add the statement "good and faithful servant,"
and she would be writing the Bible. The point is that Dagny experienced
longing, like all of us do, for an approval that goes beyond ourselves. I don't
know for sure, but I imagine that Ayn Rand expresses her own longing
through the character of Dagny Taggart. We cannot prove anything by the
existence of that longing, but it certainly leads us to look beyond ourselves
in order to be satisfied.

Likewise, Dagny looked beyond herself to find the answer to her
longing. It certainly was not to be found in Rand's dystopian society, but
it seems to elude anything in our conventional society as well. Ironically, as
we've seen with the True Atlas and the True John Galt, Rand couches her
entire answer to the problem of longing in Christian symbolism.

I can almost hear the objections from both Christians and Objectivists
at this point. John might say, "Ayn Rand knew exactly what she was doing,
and it wasn't anything but creating a hero. The similarities were intentionally included in order to add to the epic heroism." Or Dad could have
added, "Of course, growing up in St. Petersburg, she couldn't avoid the
Christian imagery that inevitably shaped her early ideas." While both of

those statements ring true to some extent, something seems to go beyond the initial intentionality. For me, that something is a longing that does not find its fulfillment in a simple reading of the New Testament or in the inspiration of a fictional character, no matter how definitively epic.

The Soul of Atlas

The title this book, *The Soul of Atlas*, draws its meaning from elements of each of my father's life perspective. The soul of something is its life force, the guts, the inside, what's really going on at the core. "Heart and soul" reflects the internal part of a person or thing. For a person, the soul is who he really is, the authentic self, his identity. It's not his body or his appearance. As important as the material can be, the immaterial aspects are what define the soul of a human being. (Even when a tumor blocks the neural activity in my eyes and ears and face, I am still me.) On a quest, the soul is the journey's purpose or climax. It's the passion fueling the ascent toward a goal. The soul of an argument is the destination, the final point or conclusion.

If Atlas represents Rand's highest ideal for mankind—the men and women of the mind who alone are the producers and sustainers of the world—then I believe the Gospel is the true fulfillment of that ideal. In short, the Gospel is the soul of Atlas.

The Fulfillment of Objectivism

True fulfillment has always been at the heart—indeed, the very soul—of Rand's philosophy. From the start, it was the aspect of her carefully articulated framework that drew me in. She opposed settling for anything short of personal happiness or non-contradictory joy. She rejected what she determined to be based on arbitrary whim or wishful thinking. I followed in her footsteps. When my intellectual journey reached a fork, the path of

Reason challenged me with the claims of Jesus and the life He offers. Both on this earth and in the future. I discovered that the truest possible fulfillment—ultimate happiness, the Joy that is permanent, life that is truest to the nature of human beings—is most profoundly understood in an intimate relationship with the One who knows me better than I know myself, and loves me more than I have ever experienced.

The highest occupation of my soul could not be anything less than the best and most glorious occupation of anyone's soul: God himself.

When my intellectual journey reached a fork, the path of Reason challenged me with the claims of Jesus and the life He offers.

Rational self-interest leads inevitably to Jesus. Furthermore, since anything less than that which is permanent ceases to have cosmic Meaning, I am settling if I focus on fleeting issues confined to a mere lifetime. And so I came to find out that the fulfillment of Objectivism is the Gospel of Jesus Christ.

12

RECONCILIATION

The analogy of the soul extends to the discussion of world views themselves. A person's philosophy flows out of the deep interior of the soul. Our world view makes our lives what they are; it fundamentally affects everything about how we live. It's everywhere. Like air or gravity, we may not even think about it, but small changes in its composition would alter our behavior. Consequently, it is crucial to understand the essence, or the soul, of any ideology: not just our own, but those that affect us. Acknowledging and understanding such influences equips us to function *with purpose*. Purposeful action, in the right context, is critical to the very achievement that imbues our lives with happiness and meaning. As I stated in the opening pages of this book, when we know what persuades us, what controls us, and what inspires us, we are able to navigate our lives with intentionality.

The Importance of a World View

Our world views comprise both private and public aspects, and we need to understand both. Furthermore, our awareness must broaden beyond our-selves to include others and how they affect us. Even the most intimate areas of life (sex, money, meaning) are also inescapably public. What I do with my money, for example, affects people around me. The spending patterns of consumers and business affect the broader economy, and the economy affects all of the citizens in a society. It pays, therefore, to understand the world views that drive these choices, since the outcomes of private deci-sions ripple through a society. Furthermore, the world views that drive the public discourse on our most private concerns have everything to do with how our liberties are protected or limited. Likewise, the most public aspects addressed in this book (Power, Capitalism, the role of government) are very personal, insomuch as very personal motivations fuel and inform them. Capitalism in the West, for example, has built the wealth of nations. Thriving in a capitalist system necessitates a choice on the part of an indi-vidual to use his mind and body to produce value.

Throughout this book, I have demonstrated that world views affect everything using the particular world views of my fathers as an example. Their guiding philosophies exemplify this private/public intertwining of ideals. And these particular ideals, I maintain, have been enormously influ-ential on our culture. Perhaps no other philosophical or ethical influences can be understood to be more quintessentially American than Christianity and Individualism. The architects of the American experiment were moti-vated by precisely these two governing principles that, at first glance, may appear contradictory. Yet individual liberty and Faith in a Sovereign Creator have endured through two hundred and fifty years of this nation's development. And so it is that any thoughtful person wishing to comprehend the "American spirit" (for better or for worse) must recognize the pervasive influences of these ideas. Moreover, in the last hundred years, these ideas come to us in even more apparently juxtaposed forms. In their contemporary incarnations, the political philosophy of Ayn Rand is a distillation of the rationalism that informed the American founders and the contemporary secular expression of their Biblical principles.

While Ayn Rand did not introduce new concepts, she codified these essentially American ideals for this post-war/cold war generation. Her brilliant reasoning stirred in the souls of her readers the imperative of individualism, fundamental truths of our existence (life, liberty, and the pursuit of happiness) and the economic liberty of capitalism that the country was founded on. In short, she illuminated that individual efforts should be rewarded in accordance with their value.

Christianity and Objectivism are predominant examples of various (apparent) philosophical "dichotomies": Reason and Faith; Atheists and Believers; Science and Religion; Individualism and Collectivism; Conservatives and Progressives. In some cases, the differences are truly irreconcilable. In others, the profound misunderstandings can be addressed directly. With some effort, seemingly opposing positions can come to terms. In *any* of these realms, there are personal and public reasons to engage in the same process that this book has undertaken: to engage, understand, reconcile, and act.

Method and Motive

The reader of this book has taken the first step by engaging. Engaging demonstrates recognition and some level of respect for the issues. Taking part in, or even initiating, the discussion establishes a platform to reach understanding. From the beginning, *The Soul of Atlas* has had understanding as its goal, not as an end, but as a means to reconciling variant philosophies. In any process of reconciliation, the parties must demonstrate understanding—to the extent of articulating the "other side" credibly—in order to reach common ground.

While reconciliation is a noble and heroic pursuit in itself, it's not a final destination. Rather, where we stand on common ground, we can act together. We can cooperate to reach goals that may be impossible to achieve otherwise.

Engage

To begin the process, we must start engaging and continue to engage. We need to converse, which begins with listening. As we articulate our own world view and accept the challenge of articulating (understanding) the other's world view, we communicate a depth of understanding. Simply put, it is important to know where others stand and the terms by which they live their lives. When we speak the same language, we have, to cite Mortimer Adler's adept phrase, "come to terms."[1] That is, when we understand the terms that the other uses and what he means by those terms, we can use them in the same context. And then we need to test out our newfound understanding. When we do, we will find common ground. It's nearly impossible *not* to find common ground where it exists and thereby find areas to celebrate.

Simply put, it is important to know where others stand and the terms by which they live their lives.

Admittedly, it can be difficult to engage where there is a high level of distrust between people. But it's imperative to trust. Why don't we? I think, mostly, it comes from a lack of understanding. Trust comes, in part, *through* understanding. I trust my son when I understand what made him do what he did. I may not like it, but I trust him because I know him. Through conversation, I begin to empathize with his intellectual, emotional, and spiritual motivations. Without understanding, trust is missing. I am left with two choices: continue in that state, or do something about it. If I didn't care about my son, I may not care enough to build a trust-based relationship. But because I do care, I want to build trust. To build trust, I need to understand.

Part of the reason we don't build trust is that we don't care enough to understand. When I am sucked up into myself, my own priorities, or my own need to be right, I often get stuck on a track. I can't seem to give up, and I hold to my point without deference to the feelings or perspective of the other person (be it my son or someone else). But it's imperative to get past the need to just be right. Sometimes being "right" counteracts our pursuit of happiness. Caring and understanding, ultimately, lead to the greater happiness of all involved. To encourage and even inspire the inclination towards understanding is the primary goal of this book.

Understand

The Soul of Atlas illustrates a particular example of "coming to understand." My need to reconcile my fathers and their ideals has driven me to actually embody this process. The inclination to *reconcile*, it turns out, was the most intentional way of figuring out what was personally important to me and to people whose world views most directly affected me. Furthermore, the process has revealed to me the imperative for empathy and understanding between any different views—maybe principally those most disparate.

Not only has the process revealed to me the imperative for empathy and understanding between variant views, but my experience has revealed important aspects of method for anyone seeking to evaluate perspectives. The four questions discussed in the second chapter ground that method: "What is the nature of Reality?" "What is a person's highest pursuit?" "What is wrong with the world?" and, "How do you fix it?" When I have engaged with an ideology long enough to hear the reasoning behind the answer to these questions, I have begun to understand. Furthermore, I strive to articulate another's view as clearly—if not more so—than it has been articulated to me. Anyone who succeeds in doing that gains credibility.

When we're addressing others' perspectives, the differences provide the biggest challenge to harmonious cooperation. But they can be addressed and the hurdles can be cleared. My successful navigation is far from complete, but the map is clear. The issues may be different depending on the world view. In the case of my fathers, the big three (Money, Sex, Power) were a logical place to start. Reason, Capitalism, and Selfishness seemed, at the outset, points of misunderstanding that begged for attention. Thinking through the perspectives and identifying where each father comes down on the issues that shape our lives provides a basis of understanding and empathy. And that's one of the most important lessons I have learned. Coming to empathize with another's point of view and being secure enough in my worth as a person to withstand the disagreements without devastating my self-esteem has been a critical skill to hone.

Reconcile

If I had not started out to find common ground—with intentionality—the goal of reconciliation would have been doomed. It was easier for me because of the emotional aspect that motivated me. I wanted, even needed, to reconcile my fathers. As a proxy for restoring their friendship, I looked to reconcile their world views. These two men, who have shaped my life more than anyone else, have been estranged by history, vocation, geography, and circumstance. The spiritual consequences at stake, from the perspective of both world views, have weighed heavily on me and pushed me to resolve the internal conflicts with a sense of urgency. I approached the quest with my mind eager to find the truth, argued with both sides in turn, and found agreement and disagreement with each. The verdict of success is not in whether or not one or the other side "won." Both win if the truth wins; both lose if one side tries to win at any price.

The journey toward reconciliation has been long. Bringing the substance of the Conversation to the written page has been cathartic for me. Understanding these two world views is an adventure in itself, but talking with my fathers about their lives and experiences is often something I take for granted. I set out to understand my fathers, and I came away with a world

> *While Objectivism and Christianity differ at their core, the logical conclusions they embrace lead to similar behavior.*

view that combines their two perspectives. The similarities and differences between these two men mirror the comparisons between Objectivism and Christianity.

Common ground. It's what I have been seeking this entire time. All of the conversations lead to this end. And what have I found? My fathers value the same entities at the end of the day. While Objectivism and Christianity differ at their core, the logical conclusions they embrace lead to similar behavior. They both live with relationships and they see the need for other people in their lives. They both want the same solutions in the realm of economics, government, and to some extent culture. But most importantly, they see the same ideas opposing their own. They know that the answer is not more government. It's not Collectivism that provides the answer, solution by committee. They may have different ideas about how to live their lives as individuals, but they want the liberty and the freedom to do that, instead of the government trying to do that for them. I now see that my fathers agree on much and could talk for hours about facets of politics, economics, and family. They agree on the morality of friendship, loyalty, honesty, and the importance of reason, philosophy, sex, and meaning. They value money, sex, and power, albeit differently in the hierarchy of their priorities and how they use them to achieve their highest value. For example, both argue for the virtues of honesty and integrity; both exalt the virtue of thinking and Reason; both argue for the exclusivity of Truth. And while they disagree about sacrifice, Faith, and tolerance, their disagreements are largely due to different definitions. Their reconciliation is literally a matter of "coming to terms."

Having said all this, the impasse is undeniable. "Christian Objectivism" or "Objectivist Christianity" is only possible by some hand waving and fabricating of definitions. Atheism and Christianity cannot both be true. Those who think that Christian Objectivism or Objectivist Christianity defines a particular world view are not defining their terms the way that Ayn Rand or C. S. Lewis would. At the end of the day, recognizing the impasses may be more of a strength than a weakness. Recognizing the limits to utter harmony is, again, a form of coming to terms.

Act

As it turns out, the places of strongest connection between these perspectives are in the political realm—ironically where no one finds common ground! So where do we go from here? As with any differing ideologies, it's impossible to proceed without understanding. In the particular case of Christianity and Objectivism, we have a foundation of understanding through the Conversation that has begun with this book. Understanding will enable us to work together through social, economic, and political influence. John is among the many individuals who have been profoundly influenced by Ayn Rand's philosophy of Reason and rational self-interest. Dad is among many who have been changed by the power of the life, death, and resurrection of Jesus Christ. These two men represent two groups of people that are foundational to conservative thought in this country. Together, and allied with other, like-minded people, they can effect great change in the world. Separately, they will continue to fight against each other. Adherents of such disparate world views can be inclined to pronouncing an all-or-nothing agenda. "You must align with me on every point or we can't work together." This just leads to alienation and failure. The enemies of objective truth, individual freedom, and limited government are too many and too fiercely opposed.

Success requires cooperation. The enormity of the task demands a rational approach. Conservatives must focus on the principles that unite them to bring about the most good for the most people. The advocates of liberty and freedom pursue those ideals in every area: worship, speech, property. In some form, these freedoms start with economic freedom, which is the right of an individual to live without his life being forcefully encumbered by other individuals. The Christian considers Jesus reaching the outcast and misfit with His grace and peace, and the Objectivist seeks production to sustain his life. Both can agree on the harmful effects of a government that overextends itself by taking these decisions away from the individual. While there are many cultural disagreements that result from engaging in conversation, that in no way negates the benefit of having the Conversation. And disparate groups *must*, in order to preserve the liberties we are afforded by the Constitution, exercise these liberties. When we do that, we may just discover more common ground. And certainly we'll set an example for others to explore Reason in place of force.

Conclusion

In the course of playing out the Conversation in my life, I have been delighted to engage with people from many ideologies, including, certainly, Christians and Objectivists. Engaging with people—locally in cafes, in home groups, informal and formal talks, and internationally through universities, business, and political organizations—I have been enriched and encouraged by the possibilities. The experience has been so invigorating, because I have learned to speak the language of varying sides, and thereby harness the intelligence and creativity of each. I wholeheartedly recommend it. May the Conversation continue.

Whether you are a secularist, a Christian, or neither, my sincere hope is that you will heed the apostle's exhortation as you consider the presentation you have just encountered.

> *Finally, brothers, whatever is true, whatever is noble, whatever is right, whatever is pure, whatever is lovely, whatever is admirable—if anything is excellent or praiseworthy—think about such things.*
>
> — Philippians 4:8 (NIV)

We can work together. When widely influential, yet substantially opposing, world views embrace the same direction, the observing world cannot avoid wonder. When we unite in our efforts and allow our agreements to take center stage, we send a signal. Together, we can advance causes that require a combined effort. Fighting over our disagreements, we expend more effort and achieve less.

Returning to the cover of this book, the scene on Fifth Avenue, the representations of Atlas and St. Patrick's Cathedral are grand, to be sure. But when all is said, they are inanimate objects that will fall into decay one day. The ideas that they represent and the Conversation between these ideas are not subject to the wear and tear of the elements. As long as thoughtful individuals pursue truth and seek happiness, the Conversation will continue. It is my hope that the richness of the Conversation will propel you to deeper understanding and *greater fulfillment in the knowledge of the truth.*

> *When widely influential, yet substantially opposing, world views embrace the same direction, the observing world cannot avoid wonder.*

AFTERWARD

A LETTER FROM JOHN

Those close to Mark, as I am, know that he is the world master in the discussion of the very important topics of Faith and Reason. This book, *The Soul of Atlas*, demonstrates that. It is an enormous undertaking, and I take great pride in his accomplishment.

I believe this book can help us re-gain our civil society. The philosophy of the extreme left and others like Islamic militants have put America's values to the test. We have placed ourselves in a position where either our values win and live on, or where, frankly, we are vanquished.

Ayn Rand said that two groups with opposing principles can never live in the same space... the stronger, more consistent competitor, will win in the end, and their way of life will survive. There can be no common ground, or negotiation, with Marxist collectivism or extreme theocracy if we want to preserve a free society.

Rand also said that opposing groups with the same principle can accommodate a "coming together" within a society. Secularists and those of faith may disagree on the existence of God, but their alliance is based upon the common values of peace, family, individual responsibility, and a limited government. Their allegiance to the virtues of "life, liberty, and the pursuit of happiness" within a civil society is their common ground.

The Soul of Atlas is an articulation of the differing views of Faith and Reason with the same principles—the goal of a society that believes in the value of the individual.

Respectfully,
John Aglialoro

A LETTER FROM DAD

Jesus says, "Seek first the kingdom of God and his righteousness." As Christians, we have a mandate to go into the all the world and preach the Gospel to every creature. To reach people, we need to go where they are; not just physically but, in this case, ideologically. Ideologically, "going where people are" means understanding. Mark's book provides just that.

The ideologies are miles apart on the surface. Mark's discussion brings out the point that political conclusions can be similar yet come from two differing theological perspectives. That similarity offers great opportunity to engage with a community of atheists that shares many of our political views.

In the final analysis it is an individual choice that each person must make for his or herself. Notwithstanding, *The Soul of Atlas* makes a special call to action so that the Objectivist and the Christian may make an inclusive rather than exclusive choice.

Warmly,
David J. Henderson

ACKNOWLEDGEMENTS

I am grateful to my colleagues and friends at Chatham Financial for their encouragement and patience as I took time off to write, especially during some of the most tumultuous capital markets in the company's history. At home, my lovely wife, Kristin, and three strapping young men—Nate, Luke, and Matt—put up with my late nights and weekends of reading, writing, and reflecting both in and out of their presence. I want to say to David, Liesl, Jordan, Justin, Valerie, Holly, and every member of the family who has listened to me go on about this book for the last five years, "Thank you."

To my supportive friends in our home group in West Chester and Kristin's Tuesday Morning group of women who pray: thanks for sticking by me during the long journey.

Thanks to my best friend and thinking partner, Scott Stanley, who gave me encouragement and many insights along the way. I can't say enough, Scott.

I am grateful to Tim and Kathy Keller for their articulation of the Gospel. They have helped me to see Jesus in an always-fresh and growing way. Tim has shown me countless examples of what it means to engage audiences in respectful conversation.

John Piper, through his book, *Desiring God*, and his balanced appreciation of Ayn Rand first opened my eyes to the possibility of disparate communities exploring common ground through meaningful discussion.

With his creative genius, Rick James took the image of Atlas and St. Pats and turned it into a beautiful cover.

More thanks than I can possibly acknowledge go to Ruth Olsen, who brought her vast editorial skill, analytical expertise and personal empathy to this project. Her work made me look like a better writer and a clearer thinker than I really am.

Finally, the entire context of this book would not have been possible without Dad, who introduced me to Christianity and Mom and John, who schooled me in Objectivism.

NOTES

TWO—TWO VOICES

1 Sire, *The Universe Next Door*, Preface.
2 Rand, *Philosophy: Who Needs It*, 8.
3 Rand, *Letters of Ayn Rand*, 356.
4 Rand, *Atlas Shrugged*, 938.
5 Ibid., 1012.
6 Ibid., 731.
7 Pascal, *Pensées*, 425.
8 Piper, *Desiring God*, 15.
9 Lewis, *Weight of Glory*, 1.
10 William Henley, "Invictus," stanza 4, in Untermeyer, 7.
11 Piper, *Desiring God*, 18 (quoting Job 22:25).
12 Rand and Peikoff, *Journals of Ayn Rand*, 90.
13 Rand, *Atlas Shrugged*, 80.
14 Rand, *The Virtue of Selfishness*, 15.
15 Rand, *Philosophy: Who Needs It*, 1.
16 Rand, *Atlas Shrugged*, 1044.
17 Rand and Peikoff, *Journals of Ayn Rand*, 73.
18 Ibid., 69.
19 Rand, *Atlas Shrugged*, 20.
20 Ibid., 21.
21 Ibid., 984.
22 Dad was quoting Psalm 27:4, (NIV).

THREE—SEX

1 Eldredge, *Wild at Heart*, 6.
2 Ibid.
3 Rand, *Voice of Reason*, 54.
4 Rand, *Atlas Shrugged*, 489.
5 Ibid., 490.
6 Ibid.
7 Ibid.
8 Ibid., 489.
9 Rand, *The Virtue of Selfishness*, 81.
10 Rand, *Atlas Shrugged*, 490.

FOUR—MONEY

1 Rand, *Atlas Shrugged*, 392, 410.
2 Ibid., 414.
3 Rand, *Atlas Shrugged*, 10.
4 Dad was paraphrasing 1 Timothy 6:10.
5 Rand, *Atlas Shrugged*, 100.
6 Philippians 4:12.
7 Stone, *Wall Street*.
8 Ibid.
9 Rand, *Atlas Shrugged*, 96.
10 The phrase, "the primacy of the individual" is one that Ayn Rand uses throughout her writing. It means that the individual comes first in the hierarchy of values, and every decision is made through the filter of whether it will enhance the life of the individual.

FIVE—CAPITALISM

1 Rand, *Capitalism*, 14.
2 Chesterton actually said, "The Christian ideal has not been tried and found wanting. It has been found difficult; and left untried." Chesterton, *What's Wrong with the World*, 37.
3 Rand, *Capitalism*, 11.
4 Rand, *Atlas Shrugged*, 661.
5 Ibid., 944.
6 Peikoff, *Objectivism*, 387.
7 2 Thessalonians 3:10 (NIV).
8 Rand, *For the New Intellectual*, 25.
9 Ibid.
10 Rand, *Atlas Shrugged*, 271.
11 Horace Bussby Mowen is president of Amalgamated Switch and Signal Company and one of Rand's villains.
12 Rand, *Atlas Shrugged*, 533. Eugene Lawson, former head of bankrupt community bank and one of Rand's villains, became a Washington bureaucrat. He expresses the un-Randian view that production is a matter of social responsibility.
13 Rand, *Atlas Shrugged*, 45.
14 Winston Churchill, November 11, 1947.
15 Peikoff, *The Ominous Parallels*, 337.
16 Rand, *The Virtue of Selfishness*, 151.
17 Ibid., 150.

SIX—REASON

1 Bacon, *The Essays*, 49.
2 Rand and Schwartz, *Return of the Primitive*, 84.

3   Rand, *Atlas Shrugged*, 982.
4   Ibid., 943.
5   Rand, *For the New Intellectual*, 128.
6   C.S. Lewis, *Miracles*, 26.
7   Ibid., 27.
8   Peikoff, *Objectivism: The Philosophy of Ayn Rand*, 48.
9   Rand, *Philosophy: Who Needs It*, 79.
10   Deuteronomy 18:22 (NIV).
11   I Thessalonians 5:21 (NIV).
12   Mary Gordon in *Bill Moyers on Faith and Reason*.
13   Peterson, *The Jesus Way*, 48.
14   Ibid., 48-49.
15   Motyer, *Look to the Rock*, 21.
16   I Corinthians 15:17-18 (MSG).

SEVEN—MEANING
1   Rand, *Atlas Shrugged*, 130.
2   Ecclesiastes 3:11 (NIV).
3   Augustine, *Confessions*, X, VIII, 15.
4   Rand, *Atlas Shrugged*, 730.
5   Ibid.
6   Ibid., 457-458.
7   Rand, *Atlas Shrugged*, 731.
8   Keller, *The Reason for God*, 162.
9   Avildsen, *Rocky*.
10   Hudson, *Chariots of Fire*.
11   Stedman, *A Victorian Anthology*, Matthew Arnold, "The Buried Life," lines 45-54.
12   Rand, *Atlas Shrugged*, 100.
13   Warburton, *Philosophy: The Basics*, 10.
14   Lewis, *Weight of Glory*, 30-31.
15   Ibid., 32.
16   Ibid., 33.
17   Colson, "A Rush of Reason."

EIGHT—SELFISHNESS
1   Rand, *Atlas Shrugged*, 285.
2   Colbert, *The Colbert Report*, March 11, 2009.
3   Rand, *The Virtue of Selfishness*, introduction, x.
4   Rand, *Atlas Shrugged*, 28.
5   Rand, *Capitalism*, 196.
6   Kelley, *Unrugged Individualism*, 6.
7   Rand, Berliner, and Peikoff, *Letters of Ayn Rand*, 287.
8   Rand and Peikoff, *Journals of Ayn Rand*, 80.

9   Rand, *Introduction to Objectivist Epistemology*, 137.

10   Psalm 115:3 (NIV).

11   Isaiah 48:11 (NIV).

12   Isaiah 43:6-7 (NIV).

13   Piper, *Desiring God*, 31.

14   "I swear by my life and my love of it that I will never live for the sake of another man, nor ask another man to live for mine." Rand, *Atlas Shrugged*, 676.

15   Mark 8:34-35. See also Matthew 10:39 and 16:24-26, Luke 9:24-25 and 17:33, John 12:25, and Revelation 12:11. (Mark 8:35) also see *Desiring God*, 199.

16   Mark 10:30 (MSG).

17   Augustine, *MignePatrologia Latina* 39, 368.

18   I Peter 3:10 (NIV) says, "Whoever would love life and see good days must keep their tongue from evil and their lips from deceitful speech."

19   Rand, *Atlas Shrugged*, 1010.

20   Rand, *The Virtue of Selfishness*, 44.

21   David Livingstone, Cambridge University, Cambridge: December 4, 1857, speech.

22   Peterson, trans. *Conversations*, 18.

23   Rand, *The Virtue of Selfishness*, 44.

24   Rand, "Causality Versus Duty," 866.

25   Ibid.

26   Ibid.

27   Lewis, *Weight of Glory*, 26.

28   John Newton, "Shall Men Pretend to Pleasure" (No.3) in *Olney Hymns*.

29   William Cowper, "No Strength of Nature can Suffice" (No. 62) in *Olney Hymns.*

30   Keller, *King's Cross*, 6.

31   Lewis, *Mere Christianity*, 175.

32   Rand, *Atlas Shrugged*, 1123.

33   Rand and Peikoff, *Journals of Ayn Rand*, 232.

34   Ibid., 285-286.

35   Lewis, *Reflections on the Psalms*, 94-95.

36   Piper, *Desiring God*, 17.

37   Augustine, *Confessions*, I.I.1.

NINE—JOY

1   Rand, *Atlas Shrugged*, 1022.

2   2 Corinthians 5:21 (NIV).

3   Rand, *Capitalism*, 133.

4   Piper, *Desiring God*, 18.

5   Rand, *Atlas Shrugged*, 1014.

6   Ibid.

7   Pascal, *Pensées*, trans. by W.F. Trotter, 113.

8   Rand and Peikoff, *Journals of Ayn Rand*, 513.
9   Rand, *Atlas Shrugged*, 1022.
10   Rand, *The Virtue of Selfishness*, 27.
11   Piper, *Desiring God*, 172.
12   Hebrews 12:2 (NIV).
13   Ephesians 1:5 (MSG).
14   Ephesians 1:9 (MSG).
15   Psalm 37:4 (NIV).
16   Piper, *Desiring God*, 24.
17   Galatians 5:22; John 15:11; I John 1:4.
18   Jude 24 (NASB).
19   Thomas Gray, Ed. Alexander Huber, *The Thomas Gray Archive*.
20   Rand, *Introduction to Objectivist Epistemology*, 45.
21   Bacon, *Meditations*, 71.
22   John 17:3 (NLV).

TEN—POWER

1   Rand, *Atlas Shrugged*, 436.
2   Orwell, *1984*, 276.
3   Shapiro, *The Yale Book of Quotations*, 490.
4   Rand, *Philosophy: Who Needs It*, 83.
5   Stossel, "The Scandal Is What's Legal."
6   Rand, *For the New Intellectual*, 15.
7   Keller, *The Reason for God*, 19-20.
8   Aquinas, *Summa Theologica*, II-II, 64, vii, ad.5.
9   Rand, *Atlas Shrugged*, 941.
10   Tolstoy, *The Law of Love and the Law of Violence*, 276.
11   Keller, *The Reason for God*, 37.
12   Rand, *Atlas Shrugged*, 735.
13   Rand, *The Virtue of Selfishness*, 61.
14   Rand, *Atlas Shrugged*, 230. (A description of Dagny Taggart, surveying the Taggart Transcontinental Line)
15   Keller, *The Reason for God*, 181.
16   Matthew 19:30 (KJV).
17   Deissmann, *St. Paul*, preface, viii.
18   Keller, *The Reason for God*, 181.

ELEVEN—WHO IS JOHN GALT? REALLY

1   Britting, *Ayn Rand*, 93.
2   Rand, *Anthem*, 108.
3   Rand, *Atlas Shrugged*, 1021.
4   Rand, Peikoff, and Schwartz, *The Voice of Reason*, 353.
5   Rand, *Journals*, 704.

6   Hebrews 12:2 (NIV).
7   Rand, *Atlas Shrugged*, 1147.
8   Augustine, *On Christian Doctrine*, I.27.28.
9   Keller, *King's Cross*, 137.
10 Rand, *Atlas Shrugged*, 455.
11 Sarin, *Left Behind*.
12 Edwards, *Works of Jonathan Edwards*, 2411.
13 Ibid., 2412.
14 Ibid., 2413.
15 Rand, *Atlas Shrugged*, 52.
16 Ibid., 220.
17 Lewis, *Weight of Glory*, 29-30.
18 Rand, *Atlas Shrugged*, 735.

TWELVE—RECONCILIATION
1   Adler, *How to Read a Book*, 96.

BIBLIOGRAPHY

Adler, Mortimer J. *Dialectic*. New York: Routledge, 2000.

Adler, Mortimer J. and Charles Van Doren. *How to Read a Book*, rev. ed. New York: Simon and Schuster, 1972. First published 1940 by Simon and Schuster.

Aquinas, Thomas. *Summa Theologica*. Translated by the Fathers of the English Dominican Province. New York: Benziger Brothers.1947. PDF, http://www.ccel.org/ccel/aquinas/summa.toc.html.

Augustine. *The Confessions*. In *Great Books of the Western World*. Encyclopaedia Britannica. first ed. Vol. 18. Chicago: W. Benton, 1952.

Augustine. *Sermon 368* from *Migne Patrologia Latina*.: quoted in John Piper. *Desiring God: Meditations of a Christian Hedonist*. Portland, OR: Multnomah Press, 1986, 241.

Augustine. *On Christian Doctrine*. In *Great Books of the Western World*. Encyclopaedia Britannica. first ed. Vol 18. Chicago: W. Benton, 1952.

Bacon, Francis. *The Essays*. Sioux Falls, SD: NuVision Publications, 2005.

Bacon, Francis. *Meditations Sacrae and Human Philosophy*. Kila, MT: Kessinger Publishing, 2000.

Britting, Jeff. *Ayn Rand*. Woodstock, NY: Overlook Press, 2004.

Chambers, Whittaker. "Big Sister Is Watching You." *National Review*, December 28, 1957.

Chesterton, G. K. *What's Wrong with the World*, San Francisco: Ignatius, 1994.

Churchill, Winston. "A Parliamentary Bill," millbanksystems.com, written November 11, 1947, http://hansard.millbanksystems.com/commons/1947/nov/11/parliament-bil

Colbert, Stephen. "The Word." *The Colbert Report*, Comedy Central. New York: March, 11 2009.

Colson, Charles. "A Rush of Reason: Anatomy of a Conversion," Breakpoint.org, written September 1988, http://www.breakpoint.org/search-library/search?view=searchdetail&id=1288

Cowper, William, "No Strength of Nature can Suffice" (No. 62) in *Olney Hymns*. Buckinghamshire, UK: Arthur Gordon Hugh Osborn, 1979. PDF, http://www.ccel.org/ccel/newton/olneyhymns.html.

Deissmann, Gustav Adolf. *St. Paul: A Study in Social and Religious History*. [S.l.]: Hodder & Stoughton, 1912.

Edwards, Jonathan. *The Works of Jonathan Edwards, Volume Two*. Revised by Edward Hickman. Carlisle, PA: The Banner of Truth Trust, 1974. PDF, Christian Classics Ethereal Library http://www.ccel.org/ccel/edwards/works2.html.

Eldredge, John. *Wild at Heart*. Nashville, TN: Thomas Nelson, 2001.

Fiss, Owen. "A Freedom Both Personal and Political." In *On Liberty*, by John Stuart Mill.

Gladstein, Mimi R. *The Ayn Rand Companion*. Westport, CT: Greenwood Press, 1986.

Godawa, Brian. *Hollywood Worldviews: Watching Films with Wisdom and Discernment*. New York: InterVarsity Press, 2002.

Gray, Thomas. *The Thomas Gray Archive*. Edited by Alexander Huber. University of Oxford. University of Oxford, Web. June 5, 2011, http://www.thomasgray.org/cgi-bin/display.cgi?text=odec#n1d.

Holmes, Arthur F. *All Truth Is God's Truth*. Downers Grove, IL: Intervarsity Press, 1983.

Hutchins, Robert M. *The Great Conversation: The Substance of a Liberal Education*. Chicago, IL: William Benton, 1952.

Keller, Timothy J. *King's Cross: The Story of the World in the Life of Jesus*. New York, NY: Dutton Redeemer, 2011.

Keller, Timothy. *The Reason for God: Belief in an Age of Skepticism*. New York: Dutton Adult, 2008.

Kelley, David. *Unrugged Individualism: The Selfish Basis of Benevolence*. Poughkeepsie, NY: Institute for Objectivist Studies, 1996.

LaHaye, Tim, Jerry B. Jenkins, Alan B. McElroy, Paul Lalonde, and Joe Goodman. *Left Behind*, directed by Vic Sarin. St. Catharines, Canada: Cloud Ten Pictures, 2001.

Lewis, C. S. *The Great Divorce*. New York: Macmillan Pub., 1946.

Lewis, C. S. *Mere Christianity: A Revised and Enlarged Edition*, with a New Introduction, of the Three Books The Case for Christianity, Christian Behaviour, and Beyond Personality. New York: Scribner, 1952.

Lewis, C. S. *Miracles: A Preliminary Study*. London: Centenary Press, 1947.

Lewis, C. S. *Reflections on the Psalms*. New York: Harcourt, Brace, 1958.

Lewis, C. S. *The Weight of Glory and Other Addresses*. San Francisco: HarperSanFrancisco, 2000.

Moyers, Bill. "Belief and Doubt," *Bill Moyers on Faith and Reason*, WNET PBS. New York: WNET, June 30, 2006.

Motyer, J. A. *Look to the Rock: An Old Testament Background to Our Understanding of Christ.* Leicester, England: Inter-Varsity, 1996.

Newton, John. "Shall Men Pretend to Pleasure" (No.3) in Olney Hymns. Buckinghamshire, UK: Arthur Gordon Hugh Osborn, 1979. PDF, http://www.cccl.org/ccel/newton/olneyhymns.html.

O'Neill, William. *With Charity Toward None.* New York: Citadel Press Incorporated, US, 1971.

Orwell, George, and Julian Symons. *Nineteen Eighty-four.* New York: Knopf, 1992.

Pascal, Blaise. *Pensées.* Translated by W.F. Trotter. New York: E.P. Dutton, 1958.

Peikoff, Leonard. *Objectivism: The Philosophy of Ayn Rand.* New York: Dutton, 1991.

Peikoff, Leonard. *The Ominous Parallels: The End of Freedom in America.* New York: Stein and Day/Publishers, 1982.

Peterson, Eugene H. *The Jesus Way: A Conversation on the Ways That Jesus Is the Way.* Grand Rapids, MI: William B. Eerdmans Pub., 2007.

Peterson, Eugene H. *The Message: The Bible in Contemporary Language.* Colorado Springs, CO: NavPress, 2006.

Peterson, Eugene H., trans. *Conversations Bible-MS: The Message with Its Translator.* New York: NavPress Publishing Group, 2007.

Piper, John. *Desiring God: Meditations of a Christian Hedonist.* Portland, OR: Multnomah Press, 1986.

Piper, John. *God's Passion for His Glory: Living the Vision of Jonathan Edwards.* Winona Lake, IN: Christian Art, 2003.

Rand, Ayn. *Atlas Shrugged.* New York: Plume, 2005.

Rand, Ayn. *The Ayn Rand Column: A Collection of Her Weekly Newspaper Articles, Written for the Los Angeles Times.* Oceanside, CA: Second Renaissance, 1991.

Rand, Ayn. *Capitalism, the Unknown Ideal.* New York: New American Library, 1966.

Rand, Ayn. "Causality Versus Duty." *The Objectivist*, July 1970, P. 866 [CD-ROM] Indianapolis, IN: Oliver Computing.

Rand, Ayn. *For the New Intellectual; the Philosophy of Ayn Rand.* New York: Random House, 1961.

Rand, Ayn. *Introduction to Objectivist Epistemology.* New York: Objectivist, 1966.

Rand, Ayn. *Philosophy: Who Needs It.* Indianapolis, IN: Bobbs-Merrill, 1982.

Rand, Ayn. *The Virtue of Selfishness.* East Rutherford, NJ: N A L, 1992.

Rand, Ayn. *Voice of Reason Essays in Objectivist Thought.* New York: New American Library, 1989.

Rand, Ayn, Michael S. Berliner, and Leonard Peikoff. *Letters of Ayn Rand.* New York: Plume, 1995.

Rand, Ayn, and Leonard Peikoff. *Journals of Ayn Rand.* Edited by David Harriman. New York: Dutton, 1997.

Rand, Ayn, and Peter Schwartz. *Return of the Primitive: The Anti-industrial Revolution.* New York: Meridian, 1999.

Shapiro, Fred R. *The Yale Book of Quotations.* New Haven: Yale University Press, 2006.

Sire, James W. *The Universe next Door: A Basic World View Catalog.* Downers Grove, IL: InterVarsity, 1976.

Stallone, Sylvester, and Oliver Stone. *Rocky,* directed by John G. Avildsen. Los Angeles, CA: United Artists, 1976.

Stedman, Edmund Clarence, ed. *A Victorian Anthology, 1837–1895.* Cambridge: Riverside Press, 1895; Bartleby.com, 2003. www.bartleby.com/246/.

Stossel, John "The Scandal Is What's Legal." Editorial. *Atlasphere Magazine,* December 28 2008, http://www.theatlasphere.com.

Tuccille, Jerome. *It Usually Begins with Ayn Rand.* New York: Stein and Day, 1971.

Untermeyer, Louis. *Modern British Poetry.* New York: Harcourt, Brace and Howe, 1920; Bartleby.com, 1999. www.bartleby.com/103/.

Warburton, Nigel. *Philosophy: The Basics.* New York: Routledge, 1992.

Weiser, Stanley, and Oliver Stone. *Wall Street,* directed by Oliver Stone. Los Angeles: 20th Century Fox, 1987.

Welland, Colin. *Chariots of Fire,* directed by Hugh Hudson. Los Angeles: 20th Century Fox, 1981.

INDEX

A

Abrahams, Harold, 122
absolutes
  morality, 26, 32, 180
  nature, 176
  Reason as, 102
  subjectivity and, 26
abstinence
  sex and, 57, 125
abstractions
  Meaning and, 117, 128
achievement
  ability and, 89, 183
  Capitalism and, 89, 176
  examples of, vii, 14, 115, 126
  Force and, 33, 173, 178
  God's view of, 37
  happiness and, 27,32, 116, 126, 142, 160-162, 207
  Joy and, 158
  longing and, 122-123
  Meaning and, 117, 118, 126, 207
  passion and, 89
  purpose and, xi
  Reason and, 56, 166, 173
  relationships and, 52, 187
  religion and, 30
  Selfishness and, 130
  self-worth and, 142, 188
  sex and, 52
  standard of, 126, 134, 142, 147-149, 196
  virtue of, 92
Adams, Samuel, 39
Adler, Mortimer, 210
adoration, *see* praise

Akston, Hugh, 182
alienation
  from God, 36-37, 41, 200
  internal, 4, 184
  relationships, 131, 150, 189, 214
Altruism
  Collectivism and, 119
  definition of, 131, 134-136, 141
  Duty and, 90
  false morality of, 5, 39, 73, 134, 142, 174
  misunderstanding of, 131
  Reason and, 145
  Sacrifice and, 135, 144
  Selfishness vs., 131
  Socialism and, 84, 85
ambition, *see* passion
Anthem, 119, 121, 195
approval
  desire for, 18-19, 35, 68, 75, 122, 197
  God's, 203
  others', 35, 134
  standards and, 151
Aquinas, Saint Thomas, 22
Aristotle, 26, 101, 133, 156-157
Arnold, Matthew, 122
atheism, 22, 209
  Meaning and, 124
  New Atheism, x, 124
  rationality of, xiv
  religion and, x, 99, 214
Atlas
  statue of, 147
  suffering of, 135
Atlas Shrugged, 48, 52
  Bible and, ix

Biblical imagery in, 203
characters
    Cherryl Taggart, 57, 134
    Dagny Taggart, 31-35, 48, 64-68, 83, 86, 116-117, 123-124, 131-134, 151, 193, 201-203
    Dan Conway, 31
    Francisco d'Anconia, 52-53, 57, 63-68, 73, 78, 123, 126, 196, 198-199
    Hank Rearden, 34-36, 48, 52, 57, 73, 86, 173-174, 196
    Horace Bussby Mowen, 90
    Hugh Akston, 182
    James Taggart, 34-36, 57, 64-65, 86, 91, 134, 174
    John Galt, see Galt, John
    Ken Danagger, 203
    Lillian Rearden, 129
    Mr. Thompson, 91
    Orren Boyle, 91-92
    Simon Pritchett, 113
    Wesley Mouch, 82, 91
economic themes in, 40
farmers in, 75
government, 174-175
heroes, 91
influence of, ix, 5
money in, 66
plot, 32, 34, 39, 174, 198
producers in, 32, 57
sex in, 52
torture scene, 195
villains, 82
Atlas
    Jesus and, 198, 200, 203
    meaning of, 198, 204, 203
    statue of, 200, 216, 217
    suffering of, 198-199, 200
Attila, 33-34, 174, 176
Augustine, 154
    "loves," 197
    Meaning and, 114
    soul, 140

authority
    absolute, 126
axioms, 104, 137, 179
    definition of, 133
    false premises and, 133, 137
    Lewis's argument for, 104
    Peikoff's argument for, 104
    Power and, 179

B

Bacon, Sir Francis, 99, 169, 179
beauty
    definition of, 117, 149
    God and, 113, 119, 165
    God's, 113, 148, 157
    hope and, xi
    longing and, 124, 202
    Meaning and, 124
    of life, x
    sex and, 55
benevolence
    Capitalism and, 85
    Duty and, 146
    Rand's view of, 85, 131
    Sacrifice and, 148
Bible
    alienation in, 41
    American founders and, 209
    Atlas Shrugged and, ix
    Ayn Rand and, 64
    Capitalism and, 84-85
    cultural influence, ix
    Dad's use of, 24, 59, 67, 84, 103
    erroneous view of, 67, 143
    human nature, 73, 85, 87
    idolatry in, 28
    Jesus and, 111
    Jesus's validation of, 110-111
    Joy and, 157, 161, 163-164
    Knowledge and, 167
    literature and, 58-59
    promises of, 186
    reading of, 137, 204

Reason and, 106-107
relationships, 144
salvation, 60
as Scripture, 54, 84, 107, 110, 137, 179
Selfishness and, 137-138, 151
sex, 54-55, 60
warnings of, 67, 106
world view, 66, 71, 79, 160, 186
Biblical references
I Timothy, 67
2 Corinthians, 185
2 Timothy, 171
Philippians, 164, 216
Psalms, 29, 41, 137, 151-152, 156, 163
Bonaparte, Napoleon, 172
Bond, James, 68
Branden, Nathaniel, 54
Britting, Jeff, 194

C

Chesterton, G. K., 37, 81, 112
Christianity
happiness and, 159
influence of, 189, 208-209
misunderstanding of, 136
money and, 88
morality of, 95
opposition to, 93
Power and, 181
Reality and, 41
Reason and, 112
sex and, 55
truth claims and, 181
Churchill, Winston, 93-94
Colbert, Stephen, 132-133
collective wisdom, 34, 36
Collectivism
business and, 83
Capitalism vs., 83. 92, 141, 209, 213
Christianity and, 31
Collective, 34-36, 41, 92-93, 131

freedom and, 131
government and, 36, 83
human nature and, 86, 93
incentives, 83, 93
individualism vs., 92
Knowledge and, 36
morality of, 83
looters and, 97
Communism
Capitalism and, 31
Power and, 174
Rand's experience of, 175
confidence
achievement and, 6
approval and, 52
argument and, 66
arrogance, 149, 158
Gospel and, 103
humility and, 164, 168, 174, 186-187
Joy and, 163
lack of, 4
self-worth, 52-53
sex and, 52
standards and, 178, 183
Conway, Dan, 31
cosmological argument, 22
counterfeit
power, 185
truth, 159
Counterfeit Gods, 159
courage
Dagny's, 132
guilt and, 155
crucifixion, 193
Corpus Hypercubus, 194,

D

Dali, Salvador, 194-195
Dawkins, Richard, x, 124
death
escapism and, 34
finality of, 110, 124, 150, 154

flourishing vs., 116
Jesus's, 23, 199, 214
morality of, 144, 174, 177
physical, 116, 150, 154
power of, 178, 185
preoccupation with, 34
spiritual, 42
suffering and, 32, 34, 121, 177
delight
God's, 137, 163
in God, 151, 156, 163
in relationships, 138, 188, 215
pleasure, 28, 153
democracy
Capitalism and, 94, 97
Power and, 173
DeNiro, Robert, 105
Dennett, Daniel, x, 124
Doctor Zhivago, 133
duty
pleasure and, 145
Dylan, Bob, 28

E

economy and economics
Capitalism, 85, 94
Collectivism, 175
free market, 81, 88, 90, 97
God's glory and, 92
government and, 83, 175
impact of, 208
laissez-faire, 97
morality and, 94
politics and, 82, 84, 94
Randian theories of, xi
turmoil in, 81
world views and, 213
Edwards, Jonathan, 199-200
egoism
definition of, 136
God and, 136
integrity, 135
Eldredge, John, 50

emotions
baggage, 4, 8
danger of, 7
emotional development, xii, 15, 210
emptiness, 156
existence of, 23, 101
Faith and, 101
greed and, 55
happiness and, 162
Joy and, 161
Knowledge and, 101, 166
longing and, 201-202
managing, 7-8, 10, 50
motivation and, 210, 212
nature of, 101
potential barrier of, 7, 14, 127
reconciliation and, 14-15, 18, 25, 48, 98, 104, 115, 141, 150-151
entrepreneurship
Capitalism and, 115
ethics
subjectivist, 31
existentialism, 30

F

Faith
acceptance and, 107
Rand's view of, 32
Reason and, x-xi, 200, 219-220
religion and, xi
revelation and, 78
works and, 57, 90, 106, 187
fascism
Christianity vs., 93
force
abuse, 174, 178, 184, 215
anti-power, 185
defending against, 177
definition of, 173
Faith and, 105
false, 185
fraud and, 95
government use of, 90, 95, 173-175

looters and, 32-34, 36, 39, 74, 95, 173-174, 176
manipulation as, 39, 176-177
mind vs., 174
money and, 72
morality of, 74
persuasion vs., 174
Power and, 186
Reason vs., 215
truth claims and, 179
voluntary exchange vs., 176
Foucault, Michel, 180-181
The Fountainhead, 152
characters
Dominique Francon, 152
Howard Roark, 152, 195-196
Francisco, *see* characters *Atlas Shrugged*
freedom
Capitalism and, 209
economic, 81, 88-89, 209, 215
Faith and, 175, 208
government and, 173, 175, 208, 213
individual and, 39, 75, 86
Joy and, 156
life and, 32, 74, 209
longing and, 50, 53
markets, 81, 86, 88, 90, 97, 175
morality of, 40
Power and, 188
producers and, 78
Reason and, 14, 42, 105
religion and, 147
Sacrifice and, 135
Selfishness and, 94
spiritual, 155-156, 208
friendship
reconciliation and, 48, 212-213
fundamentalism, 121, 177
Rand's, 178
religious, 14, 177

G

Galt, John
Galt's Gulch, 116, 197, 203

Ideal Man, 32, 196-197
identity of, 193, 195
Jesus and, 194, 196, 203
John Galt Line, 66, 201
Joy and, 161
longing for, 202-203
morality of, 196
oath of, 117, 138
passion of, 194
Rand's villains vs., 151
Reason and, 100
self-worth of, 152
soul of, 26
speech of, 32, 39-40, 86-87, 102, 141
strike of the mind and, 40, 92
torture of, 195-196
glory
Capitalism and, 86
definition of, 149
production and, 86
romantic, 48
sex and, 54
God
as First Mover, 22, 29, 41
authority of, 146
beauty and, 157
character of, 157-158
creative activity of, 14, 21-23, 28, 37-38, 41, 54-55, 60, 73, 89, 92, 113, 119, 156, 208
Duty and, 149, 156
experience of, 71
faith in,
glory of, 28, 36, 92, 138
highest pursuit of, 138
honoring, 28, 30, 54, 127
hope and, 165
idolatry and, 119
intimacy with, 39, 55, 103, 121, 138, 156, 163-165, 169
Joy and, 54, 160, 162,-164
Knowledge and, 107
longing and, 56, 90
Meaning and, 123-124, 162

misunderstanding, 30, 106
money and, 67
need for, 21, 24
personal nature of, 23
pleasure of, 159
Power and, 186
promises of, 156, 163
reality of, 21, 28, 78, 154
Reason and, 100
relationship and, 39
religion and, 12, 71, 148
Sacrifice and, 148
Selfishness and, 137-138
separation from, 42, 88, 122, 198
sex and, 55
sin and, 30
sovereignty, 134
universe and, 21-22, 109
wealth and, 67
worship of, 28, 30, 54, 151-153, 156, 163, 167
Gospel
religion and, 143, 148
see also Christianity
government
as benefactor, 39
Capitalism and, 5
democracy, 93, 173 economy, 83
force and, 95
laissez-faire, 97
policy, 65
regulation and oversight, 96, 175
role of, 5, 39, 83, 86, 90, 175, 208, 213, 215, 219
grace
acceptance and, 187
examples of, 142
God's, 60, 215
greed
Altrusim vs., 134
definition of, 65
money and, 65, 73
perceptions of, 65, 72-73
wealthy and, 64

H
Hamilton, Alexander, 39
happiness
freedom and, 42
God's, 137-138, 151, 156, 163
Joy and, 28, 157
knowledge and, 166
pursuit of, 28, 32, 166, 209, 211, 220
Reason and, 155, 160
relationships and, 138, 188, 215
virtue and, 159
heaven
conceptions of, 12, 78, 159
existence of, 146
Jesus and, 59, 79, 91
longing and, 202-203
hedonism
Christian Hedonism, 159
Joy and, 159
highest pursuit, 25, 141, 150-151
Hitchens, Christopher, x, 124
honesty, 213
dishonesty vs., 134, 151
virtue of, 213
humanity
soul of, 24-25
humility and humiliation, 35, 84, 150, 158, 164, 169, 178-179, 186-187, 194

I
identity
sex and, 59
sin and, 30
standards and, 122
threats to, 114
Truth and, 18
idolatry, 168
Bible and, 28, 120
definition of, 121
God and, 119
identity and, 5, 120
loneliness and, 57
objects of, 121

sex and, 56
sin and, 30
worship and, 152
individualism and the individual, 135,
  208-209
  Christianity and, 31, 208
  life, 25-26, 32, 36, 79, 88, 118, 131,
    133, 150
  morality, 25-26, 53, 89
  producers, 40
  rights, 31
industry
  destruction of, 32, 65
  identity and, 184

J

Jefferson, Thomas, 39
Jesus
  acceptance by, 56, 187-188
  agony of, 165, 199-200
  Altruism and, 135
  Atlas and, 198, 203
  death and resurrection, 23, 110,
    162, 196, 199, 214,
  glory of, 30
  John Galt as type, 194, 196, 203
  knowledge of, 166
  Meaning and, 148
  passion of, 194
  Rand's view of, 89, 119
  self-denial and, 27, 138
justice, 125
  God and, 137
  Power and, 184
  Sacrifice and, 141

K

Kant, Immanuel, 27, 46-47, 50, 104
  Reason and, 105
Keller, Kathy, 177, 217
Keller, Timothy J., 121, 149, 159, 180,
  184, 186, 197
Kelley, David, 135

Kierkegaard, Søren, 30, 121-122
knowledge
  encouragement to pursue, 211
  Faith and, 110
  happiness and, 166
  ignorance vs., 27, 87, 145, 166, 168,
    198-199
  Joy and, 166
  revelation and, 24, 34, 42, 109-110,
    167, 172, 174, 176-177

L

laissez-faire, 81-82, 85, 90, 92
Lewis, C. S., 27-28, 103-104, 119,
  124-125, 146, 150, 153, 202, 214
liberty, see freedom
Liddy, G. Gordon, 127
life
  affirmation of, 87
  identity and, 15, 77
  money and, 115
  virtue and, 75, 79
Livingstone, David, 143-144
loneliness, 9
  anger and, 8
  emotions, 4
  God and, 55
  hope and, 9
  idolatry and, 57
  relationships and, 50
  sex and, 49, 54-57
longing
  Atlas Shrugged, 201-203
  Bible and, 204
  C. S. Lewis and, 202
  emotions and, 18, 201
  experience of, 201-202
  God and, 90, 165
  happiness and, 159
  human, 123-125, 140, 159, 203
  implications of, 125
  Joy and, 161
  Meaning and, 125, 201-202
  object of, 58, 120

looters
    definition of, 33
    Power of, 32, 174
    producers vs., 34
    use of force, 33, 89, 174, 175
love
    acceptance and, 56
    approval and, 18
    God's, 36, 54, 60
    Jesus and, 55
    longing and, 125
    of money, 66-67, 73
    passion and, 50
    romantic, 51, 54, 115, 118
    sacrifice and, 129
    self, 26, 40, 55, 92, 117
    sex and, 56

M

Madison, James, 39
Man
    Capitalism and, 85
    created in God's image, 23, 28, 100, 119
    highest value of, 24-25, 28, 30, 54, 127, 130, 166, 182, 213
    Ideal, 92, 193-196
    nature of, 14, 28-29, 33, 36, 74, 85-87, 100, 166, 182
    rationality of, 23, 36, 74, 99-100, 174, 182
    Reason and, 21, 23, 25, 28
    uniqueness of, 28
manipulation
    Faith and, 176-177
    force and, 39
    government and, 65
    money and, 68
morality
    absolutes and, 26, 180
    Atlas Shrugged, 32
    behavior and, 31
    Capitalism and, 81, 95

definition of, 25
    guilt, 40
    happiness and, 27, 162
    individual and, 25
    mysticism and, 34
    of death, 144, 174, 177
    Reason and, 53, 86-87, 178
    relationships and, 213
    religion and, 60
    self and, 53
    sex and, 50
    standards, 60, 195-196
    virtue, 39
Motyer, J. A., 111

N

Napoleon, see Bonaparte, Napoleon
Nietzsche, Fredrich, x, 180, 186

O

Objectivism
    achievement and, 160
    Bible and, 71
    Faith and, 106, 108
    freedom and, 53
    fulfillment of, 204
    God and, 21
    happiness and, 159-160, 166, 168
    humanity and, 28
    longing and, 123-124
    Meaning and, 122, 124
    money and, 88
    opposition to, 33
    production and, 89, 215
    Reality and, 41, 126
    Reason and, 100, 102, 112
    religion and, 14, 60
    Sacrifice and, 141, 143-144
    Selfishness and, 28, 130-131
    sex and, 48, 50, 53, 55, 57
    spirituality of, 14
    standards and, 131, 150, 154
    truth claims and, 181-182

universe and, 23, 101-102
work and, 89
Objectivism: The Philosophy of Ayn Rand, 104
Orwell, George, 173

P

Paine, Thomas, 39
passion
  Christianity and, xii
  definition of, 50
  sex and, 27
  weak, 56, 189
  work and, 51
Paul the Apostle, 55, 84, 88, 106, 111,
  139, 163, 167, 185-188, 216
Peikoff, Leonard, 21, 88, 94, 104, 195
Peter the Apostle, 139
Peterson, Eugene, 109, 110, 144
philosophy
  anti-philosophy, 64
  Capitalism and, 82
  epistemology, 33
  ethics, xii, 31, 50, 68, 72, 75, 88-89,
    135-136, 142, 208
  metaphysics, xi, xiv, 23, 31
  politics, xi, 209
Piper, John, 27, 30, 137, 151, 153,
  159, 162, 164
Plato, 59-60, 197
pleasure
  Duty and, 145
praise
  Joy and, 137, 153
  misunderstanding of, 153
  Reason and, 151
  worship and, 29, 137, 139, 151, 153,
    216
prayer
  content of, 167, 169, 185
  examples of, 11, 77, 165, 167
pride
  definition of, 24
  love and, 54

self-worth, 184
sex and, 54
virtue of, 40
prime mover
  producers as, 14, 29
producers, 86
  ability, 29, 70, 72, 92, 118, 126,
    182
  create value, 14
  examples of, 57
  government and, 90
  looters vs., 64
  morality, 32
  non-producers and, 73
  prime movers, 14
  strike, 39-40
  value, 32, 34, 40
production, 87
  choice, 92
  definition of, 88
  examples of, 68
  mind and, 70
  morality, 56
  self-worth, 29
  Socialism and, 82, 90
  value, 26-30, 78, 89
  virtue, 66

R

rational self-interest
  Capitalism and, 85-86
  Christianity and, 137-138
  Joy and, 163
  producers and, 116
  Reason and, 100, 102, 214
  responses to, 140
  Selfishness as, 130
  survival and, 85
rationalism, 57
  Christianity and, 104, 107
  Faith vs., 105
Reality
  avoidance of, 8

nature of, xi, xiv, 20-21, 23, 31, 33
  truth and, 20,
Rearden, Henry,
reasoning
  abstract, 34, 104
relationship
  God and, 38, 41
relativism, xiv, 13, 181
religion, ix, 14, 32-33, 60, 65, 143,
  148, 150, 177, 185-186, 188-189
  escapism and, 152
  Gospel vs., 143, 148
resurrection, 23, 110-111, 162, 214
revelation, 44, 167, 177
  Faith and, 110, 176
  knowledge and, 24, 42
  nature of, 34
  personal aspect of, 42
  Reason and, 109, 174
  relationships and, 24
rights
  property, 33
Rocky, 122
romance, 48, 54, 124, 201,

S

sacredness
  Bible, 67
  sex and, 67
Sacrifice
  Collectivism and, 135
  definition of, 141-142, 144, 147
  Duty and, 146
  evils of, 141
  God and, 148
  Jesus and, 139
  Man and, 40
  misunderstanding of, 141, 144, 147
  self-, 26, 129, 131, 135
  worship and, 151
Scudder, Bertram, 48
self
  awareness, 74, 186

confidence, 37, 51-53, 57, 141, 145,
  150, 186, 212
  deprecation, 135, 150
  Force and, 100, 177
  gratification, 134
  narcissism, 35, 55, 85, 121, 139,
  150, 155, 165, 168
  Sacrifice and, 129, 131, 135, 140-
  141
  self-expression, 60
  selfless, 85, 134
self-esteem, 58, 173
Selfishness
  common response to, 130
  God's, 136
  misunderstanding of, 130
Shakespeare, William, 25
Sherman, Roger, 39
Sickness Unto Death, 121
sin and sinfulness, 35, 37, 135, 155,
  185, 199-200
Sire, James, 18
skepticism, 34-36, 81, 107, 166
  definition of, 166
Socialism, 85, 93-94, 175
  Altruism and, 84
  production and, 82
soul
  definition of, 26, 50, 204, 207
  existence of, 154
  Faith and, 109
  fathers', 20
  God and, 67
  happiness and, 157
  highest value, 24-25, 30, 78-79,
  133, 150, 205,
  identity and, 121
  individual and, 29, 67, 135
  longing and, 202
  material body and, 14
  Meaning and, 156
  mind and, 67
  passion and, 50
  salvation, 60, 135, 140, 154

survival, 152
value of, 154
world view and, 58
standards
approval, 151
exclusivity of, 179
identity and, 122
mind and, 52
money and, 65, 89
performance, 149-150, 184, 187
production and, 118
value and, 25-26, 34, 65, 125-126,
131, 146-147
subjectivity
absolutes and, 26
emotions and, 161
Faith and, 110
values and, 126
suffering, 125, 132
acceptance of, 161, 200
adversity, 77
avoidance, 148
death and, 177
happiness vs., 12
illustrations of, 6-7, 111, 125, 127,
165, 183
Jesus's, 195, 198-200
John Galt and, 161, 198
Joy and, 162, 164
mystics and, 34
passion and, 50
questioning, 125, 164
survival, 12

T

tolerance, 37, 76, 214
Tolkien, J. R. R., 119
torture, 194
John Galt's, 7, 161, 195-196
Power and, 173
trust
Faith and, 105, 107
knowledge and, 210

longing and, 202
money, 78
Reason, 35, 100, 107
truth claims
Christianity, 185
Objectivism, 182
Power and, 179

U

universe
justice in, 125
knowledge, 109
Meaning and, 25, 127, 205
nature of, 20-21, 23, 25, 101, 166
problems with, 30

V

value,
absence of, 29, 33, 53, 152
achievement and, 89
appreciation, 39
Duty and, 149
identity and, 152, 184
individual, 25, 53, 89, 116
life and, 195
Meaning, 124
money and, 66
permanent, 127
producing, 23, 29, 32, 68, 82, 89,
126
Reason, 42
Sacrifice and, 141-142
self-esteem, 40, 58
sex, 53
standard of, 25-26, 34, 125, 131
trading, 182-183
ultimate, 24-26, 51, 68, 136-138,
150, 154, 212
virtue, 74, 143
work and, 68, 74, 89
subjectivity and, 126
vice
Altruism as, 134, 144

definition of, 26
sacrifice and, 140-141
sex, 59, 179
sin and, 87
villains, *see* Randian villains
violence, 177
virtue, 14, 143-144
  Altruism and, 131
  Faith and, 106
  honesty and, 213
  Joy and, 159
  knowledge, 87
  life, 25, 36, 79, 88, 150
  measuring, 141
  money and, 65, 78
  production, 66, 78, 88-89
  Reason and, 56, 213
  Sacrifice and, 27, 135, 141, 152
  Selfishness as, 39, 94, 130-133
  work, 88-89
The Virtue of Selfishness, 130, 140

W

Warburton, Nigel, 123
weakness, 53
  Christianity and, 60, 185-186
  desires, 27, 56, 147
  fear and, 12, 49
  passion, 27, 147
  government redistribution
    of, 60
  standards and, 65
Witch Doctor, 33-34, 176
work
  Capitalism and, 5
  Meaning and, 89
  money and, 74
  virtue of, 68, 75, 88-89
world views, 18
  influence of, ix
worship, 5, 8, 28, 39, 56, 120, 124,
  151-153, 163
  delight and, 153
  oneness and, 154

ABOUT THE AUTHOR

Mark David Henderson graduated from Brown University, where he studied Victorian poetry and neuroscience. He received a master's degree in business from Columbia Graduate School of Business in 1998. He has worked in commercial banking, investment banking, and asset management. He is an engaging speaker on a variety of topics including economic, social, and cultural considerations of Faith and Reason.

Mark is thrilled he finally took enough time out of his capital markets career to write a book about his greatest passion... truth. Though his heart will always be in New York City, Mark, his wife, Kristin, and his three sons have happily settled in rural Pennsylvania. Wherever you find Kristin, you will also find Hunter, their Goldendoodle, gnawing on one of Mark's shoes.

FOR MORE INFORMATION

If you would like to continue the Conversation, consider engaging with like-minded enthusiasts on *The Soul of Atlas* blog:

http://www.soulofatlas.com

On the blog, we explore all of the topics in this book and many more, with a focus current events, politics, and culture. You will find provocative and insightful dialogue with people of varying perspectives and stay informed about speaking events, conferences, and other opportunities to engage.

Join us on Facebook at http://www.facebook.com/SoulofAtlas

You many also follow the author on Twitter @MDHenderson

Don't forget to check out http://www.ReasonPublishing.com for more titles from Reason Publishing.

23179526R00155

Made in the USA
Lexington, KY
30 May 2013